Other Books by
MEL MARSHALL

How to Fish: A Commonsense Approach
 (Winchester, 1979)
Buffalo Hunt (Ballantine, 1975)
Steelhead (Winchester, 1973)
Drift Fence (Ballantine, 1971)
Cooking Over Coals (Winchester, 1971)

SIERRA SUMMER

BY MEL MARSHALL

University of Nevada Press   Reno, Nevada, 1979

Library of Congress Cataloging in Publication Data

Marshall, Mel.
  Sierra summer.

  1. Sierra Nevada Mountains—Description and
travel. 2. Natural History—Sierra Nevada Moun-
tains.
I. Title.
F868.S5M37   917.94'4'045   79-4174
ISBN 0-87417-053-2

University of Nevada Press, Reno, Nevada 89557 USA
© Mel Marshall 1979. All rights reserved
Book designed by John Sullivan
Printed in the United States of America

For Aldine, of course, who knows the Sierra; but also for Carla, Connie, and Evan; Frank; Jim, young Frank, and Lee; they are its future custodians.

CONTENTS

S THE EASONS

In the high country of the Sierra Nevada Mountains there are only two seasons: winter and summer.

Along the 450-mile spine of the towering narrow range, summer unfolds with swift dramatic progression, and its duration is measured in days. The full impact of the brief summer is greatest above the mile-high altitude mark, and on those who have watched winter seize the mountains with one quick blast of biting winds and driving snow, then returned nine months later to see the cold season release its grasp with the same kind of rushing changes that marked its onset.

Above 7,000 feet, in what is called the high country, vegetation and animal life burst into maturity, decline, and then disappear within a span of a hundred days. Summer asserts itself with the same sudden authority that winter did. Neither season gives long forewarning of its intention to invade the heights above the snow line.

Despite geological differences between the eastern and western flanks of the mountains, the snow line occurs on both sides at roughly the same altitude, about the 5,000-foot level. Above this point the ground remains snow-covered throughout most of the winter, after the first major storm. Below the snow line the earth will be whitened intermittently but generally remains bare through the winter; its appearance changes little with the seasons. This is foothill country.

To most of those familiar with the range, the mountains begin at 5,000 feet, in forests of conifers broken by green meadow areas. Between the 6,000- and 7,000-foot levels raw granite and basaltic ridges begin to appear with increasing frequency, and at 9,000 feet, where the High Sierra begins, granite dominates.

In the high country there is no soft leisurely awakening of spring, no long weeks of mellow autumn. At 7,000 feet and higher the seasonal transitions are abrupt. Summer yields

A late winter storm seizes the mountains with one last blast of biting winds and driving snow.

without warning, usually before the beginning of October, when stratified high-flying moisture-laden clouds ride in from the Pacific Ocean, 150 miles west of the Sierra. Twenty to thirty thousand feet aloft, these clouds collide with a steady stream of warm air sweeping up from the arid broken country that lies in the shadow of the mountain's precipitous eastern face. Penetrating the clouds, the warm air dissolves them so close to the peaks that the moisture created by their dissolution does not have time to liquify into rain during its short journey downward. It falls as snow on the escarpments already chilled by a succession of freezing nights.

Early snowfalls in the high country are composed of large, thick, moisture-heavy flakes. Later, after the desert air cools, the snow will be powderlike, often sand-fine, but some of the early season snowflakes are the size of silver dollars. Once it has fallen, lodging on the precooled granite of the upper levels, the early snow seldom melts completely, as do most first snowfalls in kinder climates. It stays, clinging to the ridges. The new snow soon covers the streaky remnants of last winter's pack which, ice now more than snow, have survived as subminiature glaciers in rocky crevices. Snowfall follows snowfall from October until May and the drifts rise up. In places they will tower sixty feet or higher before winter ends.

Although the white surface seems to hide a land that can only be dead and sterile, the high country lives during this time, but with a slowed pulse. The deer have left, except for a scattered few that will remain to brave the barren season. At the first late-summer storms the herds migrate to graze through the winter in grassy valleys below the snow line. Bears, fat after weeks of constant foraging, remain in their rocky clefts and caves for progressively longer periods until they fall into the semi-stupor of hibernation. Even before the first snows, badgers and marmots have curled up in their underground dens to begin a long winter sleep. With their ponds sealed by a thick coat of ice, beavers move from their stream-bank burrows only to swim under the ice to the pond bottoms where they have stored their winter food: bark and twigs stripped from willow and aspen branches.

Chickarees do not hibernate; they laze away the cold short days and prolonged nights, spending most of their time in warmly lined tree-hollow nests, feasting off the pine seeds they harvested and stored when the weather was warm. Field mice and shrews shelter in deadfalls. Woodrats sleep in burrows under the domed nests they constructed painstakingly during soft summer nights. Chipmunks and ground squirrels scamper along the intricate maze of passageways that make up their underground tunnel-cities and live off their hoards of summer-gathered seeds.

A close look at the snow's surface, especially before the crust forms after a fresh fall, tells the story of other lives in the mountain winter. The trough of a porcupine's tail dragging through the snow between its toed-in pawprints traces porky's leisured progress from tree to tree. Muffled blotches left by a rabbit's winter-tufted pads may be overlaid by the sharper-cut prints of a stalking predator: the spaced paw-marks of a coyote or fox, the pugmarks of a bobcat, and less often, those of a cougar. More common are the narrow long-clawed prints of smaller feral animals: weasel, mink, marten, fisher. Rarely, there may be the dainty starred prints of a mountain fox, smaller prints than those of the lowlands breed.

Invisible under the snow-crust are the miniature trails, runs and tunnels made by deer mice and shrews, by voles and their small fellows. Hidden also are the extensions of underground tunnels that pocket gophers and ground squirrels make between soil and snow. These runs form a secret network below the hard opaque crust, connecting nests and burrows with food caches and water. Occasionally, in places where the snow lies thin, a ragged crater will appear overnight, marking the place where a meat-hungry coyote or bobcat has broken into a tunnel in search of a midnight meal.

There are other signs of life and death on the snow's surface. Sharply defined parentheses cut by wing-edges bracket the spot where an owl wintering above the snow line has swooped down in deadly foray. Where the snow is ridged in a semicircle by ruffled smudges, a hawk has dropped to pick up an unwary mouse or chipmunk. Long parallel streaks, wide apart, tell where the hindpaws of a bobcat skidded when it launched itself in a spring. A line of regularly-spaced pockmarks ending in a scruffy patch of disturbed snow are the pawprints of a weasel bouncing in its hopping, sinuous gait to overtake a luckless small animal.

Suddenly one day, the snow holds no tracks. The temperature has reached that stage of delicate balance at which each day's sunshine liquifies the crust and each night's chill refreezes the surface before the animals emerge in the twilight to move about. When this temperature balance arrives, there will be no overnight fall of powder snow to cover the crust and preserve fresh patterns of trails etched by small scurrying feet. This is the first sign that summer has arrived.

Under the snowpack, the springs have flowed all winter and fed a trickle of water into the creek beds, but these small streams have run unseen. At summer's onset there is a subtle warming of the air, though it is not yet prolonged enough to break winter's grip and call attention to the season's change. The warming is imperceptible to human senses, and can be measured only on the most sensitive thermometers in tiny fractions of a degree, but it is there. The daytime air no longer penetrates deeply enough into the snowpack to chill the surface of the streams. The water's warmth is now enough to melt the snow directly above its course, and the small creeks cut tunnels under the softening snow.

Creases appear in the crust and trace the waterways, and soon the rills and runs begin to show through the sagging indentations as dark lines woven through a landscape still white and hidden. Threads when they first become visible, their courses suggested only by vague wavy grey-black lines below the surface, these little streams grow quickly. The same warming that has freed their waters has touched the earth and the rocks that stud it; these, too, begin to give off heat. The tall pines feel the change. Sap starts to rise from their roots, warming the tree trunks from within. Around the rocks and trees the snow softens and droops. Where creeks run the snow crust sags until valleys form in the surface above the stream beds.

As soon as the sagging crust touches the water, it begins to melt. Its moisture merges with the running creeks and feeds them. The streams grow and rise and wash away more snow. Their currents quicken, lay bare the boulders and gravel bars in their beds. Eddies form in the shallows along the banks and strip the snow away. The streams emerge, already singing their murmuring summer melodies.

Once this first change has taken place, there is no long period of transition, no perceptible warning, no soft spring breezes to carry fresh scents of budding plants. Summer arrives as quickly as winter did, but the season's change cannot be felt yet or sensed, it can only be seen. The air stays cold, the nights bring fresh freezing. The body of the snowpack appears undisturbed, a thing of permanence, immutably fixed on the mountainsides, but to an observer familiar with the high country, the days of winter and snow have now ended.

Summer's arrival first becomes visible in the snowpack as it gives grudgingly to the new season. Only the crust melts, and then only at midday for a brief period. There is a change in its surface look, however; the crust loses its opacity and becomes translucent. Below it, the thick layer of the pack is melting, rotting, softening, and each day the crust stays fluid

For a brief time a stream flows in each meadow, fed by the shimmering thin sheets of water that pour over grassy ledges.

for a longer time. By the first week of June the temperature
reaches its day's peak not at midday, but by midmorning, and
when this time arrives the entire mountain range presents
new vistas of sight and sound.

Dulled human senses, unattuned to the transformation
that is taking place, are first alerted to the change by sound
alone, the sound of moving waters. In the early morning the
sighing of melting snow running through meadow-channels
to flow down the slopes murmurs like a breeze rustling in the

Meadow rills merge and widen at low points, forming snow ponds that may stand through much of the short summer.

pines. The treetops are motionless, though, and no air currents brush over exposed skin. Suddenly the realization comes that the all-prevailing, persuasive sound that fills the air is not that of wind, but of rushing water.

Once begun, the change moves rapidly. Pines drop their snowcaps, boulders appear protruding wetly black, the sagging creases that have been traced earlier on the snow's white surface emerge as streams. The snow slips in great masses off raw granite domes; it slides down screes that slant sharply at the bases of crags and bluffs, and the melt-water spins shining threads down steep canyon walls into the rising brooks. Except for sheltered drifts in the lees of ridges, in deep crevices of rock, and in groves where pine and fir branches interlace almost inextricably, the snow goes completely within a few days.

For a brief time a stream flows in each meadow, fed by the shimmering thin sheets of water that pour over grassy ledges. Usually the meadow rills merge and widen at low points around the clearing's edge, pouring always downward, seeking the lakes and big rivers that lie below the peaks, but this does not always happen. In saucer-formed meadows the rills run inwards and blend their courses to cover the meadow completely, washing to its edges the litter of last summer's dried stalks and stems and leaves. In such meadows, from which the water can find no ready outlet, the melt-water forms snowponds that may stand through much of the short summer.

Deeply-saucered meadows that will support such ponds are rare, however. From most of the grassy flats the rills run into creeks, and the creeks feed the rivers, which grow deep and broad, swift-currented and turbulent. Where streams have cut paths through narrow valleys that end with sharp drop-offs, they plunge over vertical cliffs, and waterfalls appear. Most of the falls live only a few weeks, white frothy swathes against grey granite walls. Soon they diminish to trickling threads or disappear entirely.

There is still snow, of course, in the high country. Summer's progress in the Sierra can be measured by recession of the snow line. Where it begins, at about 5,000 feet, the melt

Most of the falls live only a few weeks, white frothy swathes against grey granite walls, soon diminishing or disappearing entirely.

moves upward nearly a foot a day. At 6,000 feet, the melt's progress is halved; another thousand feet higher and it is reduced to four inches daily. Even under bright beating sunshine the melting at 8,000 feet measures a scant three inches a day, and where the High Sierra begins at 9,000 feet, the melt's upward progress is measured in fractions of an inch each day, even in midsummer.

In the high country the three- to six-inch daily melt actually moves more quickly than average figures indicate. Fed by newly tumultuous creeks, the lakes rise. The snow lining their banks is undercut and breaks off in massive chunks that quickly disappear in the rising water. The sun glows warmly from the instant it rises, and its unshaded glare heats the raw granite ledges; its beams creep through the most densely tangled branches. Under the trees, snow still covers the ground, but its surface has undergone a change; it is no longer virgin white as it was during the winter. In the forest it is strewn with twigs and pinecones and needles; on the meadows, where warmer earth temperatures have started the melt from below the flabby crust, thousands of dark dots pock its once white expanse. These are the tips of new grass blades protruding above the sagging crust, carrying the warmth of fresh sap in their slender stems to speed the melting process still more.

It is summer and azaleas and whitethorn and buckbush begin to grow while snow still buries them. Black-eyed Susans crowd the rocky slopes (left). New shoots race old in speeding up from the twisted willow-roots. Buds like spiny footballs form on the smooth bark (right).

The mountain meadows are unveiled, already green. Skunk cabbages thrust their phalliform tips up from the edges of the snow ponds.

Within a week after the temperature balance shifts, it is summer. The mountain meadows are unveiled, already green; while the snow was softening, fresh green blades were pushing upward under its crust, between the roots of last summer's yellowed stalks. The grasses grow with such speed that the intense green tips of coarse squawgrass rippling in the breeze often hide melt-water still standing a foot or more deep on the earth which grass now covers. The azaleas and whitethorn and buckbush begin to bud while snow still buries them and their new leaves are unfolding above the white patches that remain around their roots. Skunk cabbages thrust their phalliform tips up from the edges of snow-ponds, and currant bushes send their new runners out under the water that covers the ground.

At meadow borders the aspens have begun extending soft new twigs, bumpy with buds from which leaves soon unfold.

Upslope from the aspens branch tips of the pines have shot straight up, and each pine takes on the look of a candle-decorated Christmas tree. Across meadows and along valleys where creeks course or springs rise or lakes shelve into shallows, fresh twigs stretch up through the bare ochre limbs of willow clumps. New shoots race old in speeding up from the twisted willow roots as melting snow sends water seeping down through the rootlets and the sun darkens the pale new growth until it quickly matches the warm brown of last year's branches. Overnight the willow sap rises. Buds like tiny spiny footballs form on the smooth bark within a day's time; within a week each pod will burst into an amorphous mass of clumped feathery seeds impatient to blow away and begin clumps of their own.

Where forest fires have burned, sometimes a century or more ago, chinquapin and juniper and manzanita show fresh leaves at the first warming touch of sunshine. These are cautious plants, and their leaves emerge deliberately, as though ready to retreat if an unseasonal snowstorm should pass and nip them. The leaves are almost invisible when they first appear, tentative pale slivers, nearly transparent, hiding at the nodes of the branches. When the melt gains headway and the air grows warm, the leaves pop open like uncoiling springs. In a few hours on a sunny day the barren shrubs grow green between the skeletons of still-standing fire- blackened snag trees.

At the upper edges of the high country the melt is slow, for summer hesitates at 8,000 feet, stumbles and occasionally retreats at 9,000 and virtually halts above 10,000. Most of the snow, however, will eventually slide off the warming granite tors whose jagged profiles shove above the rounded domes that dot the mountain peaks. Even here the season's change is not denied. On the raw rock that shows above the snow the dull lichens glow with new life as if these most primitive of all Sierran plants draw a revival of growth from the summer that is unfolding so rapidly below.

In the high country the beginning of the melt always brings out snow plants. These are saprophytes, with shallow roots bedded only in the duff, that floor of decaying humus that covers the ground between the pines. Snow plants send up rose-pale stalks through the melting snow and as the actinic quality of the sun's rays increases folded buds along the stalks burst open and expand into fleshy petals of brilliant purple-red. Given perfect conditions of light, temperature and moisture around their roots, snow plants may live a week or longer, but sometimes their translucent flowers grow dark and shrivel within a day or two; often they are at their greatest beauty for a span of only a few hours.

Far downslope, where snow does not cling in winter, the cycle of seasons is the reverse of that found in the high country. In the soft air of the gradually sloping western foothills, spring creeps up from the valleys in March, and wildflowers grow to their full development between the digger pines and pin oaks long before the high mountain summer has begun. On the more abrupt eastern escarpment, the high desert country below the peaks has known only dry cold during the winter. Its clumps of sagebrush and sandgrasses show little change in winter or summer. Below both flanks of the range, though, there are four distinct seasons. Only the high country races through a summer that is born matured from a long winter, and that is counted in days rather than months.

There is something frighteningly spectacular about summer in the Sierra Nevada heights. Between the 6,500- and 9,000-foot levels it is quite literally possible to watch the budding, maturity and death of plant life almost as these would be seen in an arrested-motion camera study. Animals, too, share the urgency of the short season, which compresses into ninety or one hundred frost-free days the growth that in a milder environment would be spread over nearly half a year.

This explosion from frozen white sterility into sudden life is not unique to the Sierra, of course. Other ranges and climates where winter sets in early and holds long show similar, perhaps almost identical patterns. What is unique about the Sierra Nevada, and distinguishes this range from others, is that its heart lies so close to its feet. To reach the center of other great ranges it is necessary to travel many miles through constantly rising foothills. Midpoint in these

At meadow borders the aspens have begun extending soft new twigs, bumpy with buds from which leaves soon unfold.

more sprawling ranges is reached so gradually and is surrounded so completely by broad-based, valley-isolated peaks that the middle of the range somehow seems diminished in importance, lessened in impact. This is not true of the Sierra Nevada. The high country that is its heart lies within a relatively narrow span of miles, but despite its easy accessibility, those who reach it have no doubt that they have arrived at the true heart of the range.

An important aspect of the Sierra's heart is that in an era when civilization is encroaching with quantum leaps on all things natural, the Sierra high country is touched by very few people during the brief interval between snows. The mountains have been scarred, are being scarred, by man's use over a span of two centuries, but their heart remains much as it was when men first visited it. The innermost places appear calmly imperturbable to the casual passerby, yet reveal a pulsing inner life to those who take the trouble to pause after they have reached the heart.

Since men first became aware of the Sierra Nevada in 1772, dozens of books have tried to present the grandeur of the range. Some of these simply view the scenic vistas with hushed awe, others present specialized viewpoints. Books have been written by geologists, biologists, etymologists, botanists, ichthyologists, folklorists, engineers, historians, conservationists, hunters, fishermen, mountaineers. These have detailed minutely each aspect of the Sierra's 450 miles of peaks and valleys and mountain meadows, streams and lakes, animals and plants and birds with varying degrees of insight and excellence. The range has always been a magnet for writers; the Spanish priest who was the first white man to see the Sierra filled pages of his diary with notes and sketches, although he got no closer to the mountains than a hundred miles.

This book will take you closer, but it is not one of specialized knowledge. You may find in it conclusions at variance with the findings of scientists who have dissected the range with cold dispassion. Look for no yarns of hunting or fishing or camping, though these inevitably will be mentioned. Do not expect high adventure. No maddened grizzlies or snarling mountain lions will be pursued or faced down or dropped with a rifle bullet. It does not take you to the High Sierra, where granite crags are scaled with piton and karabiner at stupendous risk to life and limb. There are animals in the book, but they will not act or think like anything except animals. There are also a very few people in the book, but none of them will be supermen performing superhuman feats. The people are incidental; so is the narrator.

What this book does attempt is to preserve—perhaps more accurately to evoke—the summer season in one small pinpoint of the huge Sierra Nevada panorama. The summer is distilled from many summers, and the pinpoint would be smaller than a flyspeck on a map drawn to average scale. Actually, the pinpoint is an area roughly ten or fifteen miles in diameter, its center a camp beside a lake that will be nameless.

Within this small compass the entire Sierra high country is typified; it is the inner heart of the Sierra's heart. Inside the circle, the trees and plants, birds and animals, the rocky outcrops and meadows, the water, soil and weather are distinguished more by their similarity to rather than their variance from other parts of the range. Inside this circle all the significant Sierran lives meet and overlap and mingle. Its limited area contains and reveals all the many aspects of the entire range; it is this microcosm that illuminates and reveals the whole.

And perhaps this book is more: an attempt to preserve, not altogether unselfishly, that small radius as it has always been but some day may no longer be. And the book may also be written with the hope that an understanding of what such a limited area can offer will encourage others to seek and find similar unspoiled places and to fight for their preservation in some Sierra of their own.

L THE AKE

TWO

Inside the somewhat arbitrarily drawn ten- or fifteen-mile radius of the circle that typifies the Sierra high country there are about a dozen lakes of all sizes and shapes, so the name of the small lake that lies at the circle's center is not important. The lake does have a name, but the name, like the outline of its contours, will be found only on maps drawn to an exceedingly large scale.

Those interested enough to seek out such a map can learn the name and precise location of the lake without much effort, or they can find another enough like it to be its twin. Anyone taking this much trouble can be trusted to treat the lake and its surroundings with kindness and understanding. Those driven only by curiosity to visit it will not bother to search for the necessary information, and the idly curious would almost certainly lose interest when they learn that they cannot drive on a paved road to the lake's shore.

No highway leads to the lake. The pavement ends twenty miles from it, chuckholed pavement of a road that has grown progressively more narrow and winding. From the end of pavement a washboard gravelled road with many forks must be followed. The gravelled road wanders casually. For the first half-dozen miles after the pavement ends, it goes through more meadows than forests, and the pines that border it are small. Here, a great fire seared the earth bare more than a half-century ago, and the forest has been slow to recover. The pines are coming back, though. So are the aspens, their leaves dancing bright green and olive-silver when a breath of breeze passes in the early summer and shimmering orange-gold at summer's end.

We do not follow a single road to reach the lake, but many. The gravel road forks at surprisingly close intervals and most of these forks lead to dead ends, either a pair of impassable grown-over eroded ruts or a box canyon where it stops abruptly at the base of a sheer cliff. Some of the forks go as far as a jumble of weathered timbers where a mine was abandoned. Others switch back and forth to climb valley sides to the edge of a long-ago lumber stand where further progress is halted by the bole of a large tree felled across the rutted path. Two or three of the forks simply fade away in the deep grass of broad meadows, and at least two of them curve back to rejoin the pavement. To reach the lake which is the center of our Sierra summer it is necessary to know, each time a fork is encountered, which direction to take. To the stranger all the forks look alike.

In the course of thirty summers that have passed since my wife and I first came upon the lake, we have explored the forks that branch off the lazy gravelled road. This exploration has not led to any earth-shaking discoveries, but has never failed to reveal things overlooked by the hurried traveller who is interested only in getting from one point to another with the greatest possible speed over a well-paved highway.

Slow back-road travel reveals ramshackle shanties, many of them leaning crazily and appearing on the verge of collapse, but which somehow seem to remain standing year after year. Some, those at meadow-edges, are still used a few weeks each summer by sheepherders who have brought flocks to graze the mountain meadows, or by ranchers summering cattle in the grassy spots. Close watching discloses traces of long-abandoned railroad lines, built before the days of gasoline to haul logs from the mountain flanks to mills in the valleys. Along them are rotting ties and rusted scraps of metal from flatcars or engines, a cracked discarded gear from a Shay locomotive, the screen-fringed rim of a spark arrester. On meadows and beside streams an occasional splintered ox-yoke can be found, or the split planks of a sluice box or flume, a broken sun-purpled bottle, the bottom of an earthenware crock, the chewed remains of a leather boot-sole. Almost everywhere through the Sierra there can be found similar decaying reminders of the men who have labored there, or just passed through.

Along the road-forks there are snowponds the size of small lakes; springs gushing unpolluted water that tastes of minerals from the earth's heart, and free of the chemical flavor of the recycled water drawn from city pipes. This water is as different from that of civilized places as a fine vintage claret that has been carefully cellared for a decade is different from last year's raw pressings of a vineyard. Civilized water is thin and flat, that from high-country springs has the tang of carbonation without the bubbles. Water from city mains is standardized, its chlorine flavor is monotonous, pallid and flat. Water from mountain springs has individuality.

Those who came often to the Sierra in days when salt and pepper and spices were expensive and used sparingly had unspoiled palates. They could identify by taste the water from different springs. Regular travellers would make special stops to replenish their kegs or canteens from a favorite spring, bypassing others. Mountain spring water diminishes in quality, however, when it is stored; after a few days of confinement in a jug or bottle its tang fades. There seems to be a symbiotic relationship between high-country springs and their surroundings.

Always along the untravelled forks there are animals. In small meadows deer look up from grazing, freeze to immobility, ready to run in their singularly ungraceful bounding way if we stop too near them. If we keep our distance, the deer usually stalk off with slow dignity, ignoring our presence. In roadside clearings marmots sun themselves on rocks or on the weather-silvered boles of fallen pines, and squint at intruders like old men peering through badly fitted bifocals. Among the trees chickarees dart, and chipmunks. If the day is very early or very late there may be a glimpse of a cougar's tawny flanks between the pines, or the crackling of underbrush that accompanies the sudden bolting of a bear, or the fugitive sight of a marten's tawny back. A porcupine may poddle across the vestigial road in front of us, taking its time, unafraid and unhurried.

Both the main gravelled road and those forking off it meander through valleys, deep and shallow. The roads climb in and out of the valleys in roundabouts and switchbacks across the shoulders of progressively steeper ridges. There are slopes where pines grow as they have from the forest's beginning, untouched by the logger's saws. From ridges that overlook such slopes as these, the eye cannot penetrate the thick maze of close-spaced trunks and interlacing limbs. Only occasionally, where the ridges are very high and the slopes below them very steep, is it possible to look through the treetops and glimpse a small peaceful meadow or the glint of a vest-pocket lake or big snowpond, and to look across the valley to another slope as thickly forested.

As the altitude increases the nature of the forest changes. The aspen groves thin to a few scattered trees at meadow

Railed bridges between cracked concrete buttresses give way to twin-tracked crossings made from heavy timbers spiked to logs.

Creeks run across the road and the traveler gets used to the noisy splashing and grinding of car wheels on wet gravel.

rims. The brown striated trunks of Douglas firs appear among the honey-gold tortiseshell bark of big yellow pines. The creeks grow smaller and the bridges across the creeks change character. Railed bridges between cracked concrete buttresses give way to twin-tracked crossings made from heavy timbers spiked to logs; some of these, long unused, have sagged and cracked and fallen into the stream beds. Only in late summer can these creeks be crossed, bypassed on a detour near the bridge where low banks make fording the stream possible. Eventually there are no more bridges. The creeks run across the road, water crossings that must be traversed; the traveller gets used to the noisy splashing and grinding of car wheels on wet gravel.

Here, a score of miles from the end of pavement, it is necessary to look closely, and then to look a second time, to find elements alien to nature. Where summer is of such short duration those who use the land in its hundred snow-free days leave few marks. The number of users is scanty: a rancher grazing cattle or sheep in one of the bigger meadows, an occasional timber crew, a party of anglers come to stay the weekend, hunters at summer's end, a solitary backpacker. All are passersby, not dwellers.

In this part of the Sierra there are few year-round residents; they are found only in the small isolated towns that cluster beside the rare paved roads. The mountains' eastern slope is the heart of the high country. It has changed little since the earth buckled and folded to form the range, since white-hot gouts of magma came boiling up from its molten center to create other peaks and ridges thousands of centuries ago; since the grinding upheavals stopped, since the magma cooled and nature's work of making the range habitable began.

Officially, the Sierra Nevada range begins at the fortieth parallel of latitude and ends 350 miles south at the thirty-fifth parallel. The decision limiting the range was a political one made in Washington, D. C., and it was one with which many leading geologists of the day did not agree. The debate over setting boundaries for the Sierra went on for many years, and before it ended had touched on the entire interrelated chain of mountains that begins in Alaska and runs almost uninterrupted across two continents, to the tip of South America.

Understandably, most of the debate revolved around that part of the extensive series of mountain formations that lie inside the United States. There were arguments over basaltic versus granitic formations; over volcanic versus seismic origins; over typical flora and fauna; over whether the name "Sierra Nevada Mountains" should be given to the single long span between Canada and Mexico, or whether to divide the span into several ranges and name each separately. Complicating the technical details were geological and biological facts, as well as emotions.

Both basaltic and granitic formations, peaks created by both volcanic and seismic forces, occur along the entire span. The plant and animal life throughout the U.S. portion of the mountains have more similarities than differences when

The mountains' eastern slope is the heart of the high country, little changed since the geologic age when earth buckled and folded to form the range.

allowances are made for the effects of altitude and for the diverse character of adjacent alluvial valley and high desert terrain on the mountains' environment.

Personal beliefs replaced scholarly research and grew into prejudices; then prejudices flared into enmities as the arguments dragged on. All the enmities and harsh words and specious circumlocutions are best consigned to history and buried, as have been all the individuals involved in the debates. We need to note here only that during the controversy of the late 1860s, many geologists and naturalists held—and a few still privately hold today—the opinion that the correct point of division of the range, the true beginning of the Sierra Nevada, is at the northern base of Mt. Shasta, sixty-five miles above the fortieth parallel.

Politics prevailed to cut the controversy short, and the fortieth parallel was established as the northern limit of the Sierra and the southern boundary of the Cascade Range. In spite of this official decision, many old-time residents of the Shasta-Lassen areas still think of themselves as living in the Sierra rather than the Cascades.

If a measurement is made in a straight line between the tallest peak of what many still believe to be the natural northern boundary of the Sierra, Mt. Shasta, to the highest southern peak, Mt. Whitney, the lake at the center of our imaginary circle in the range is within a dozen miles of being exactly midway between the two highest peaks. It is also at the midpoint of altitude of these two great mountains, both of which tower more than 14,000 feet above sea level. The lake's surface lies at 7,640 feet. There is a third dividing line, that location in any mountain range where neighboring streams flow in different directions to separate watersheds.

In the Sierra Nevada, these drainage lines run primarily east and west. The lake's small oval valley flattens a jutting ridge with slopes that drop away from it on both sides. On the western slope, the streams flow by various devious or direct routes into the Yuba River, which in turn joins the American, which flows into the Sacramento, which empties into the Pacific Ocean through San Francisco Bay. On the ridge's eastern slope, the creeks tumble into the high desert country of Nevada as well as into the Little Truckee River, all of which—in ways more devious than those of the western slope—ultimately find their ways into the Humboldt Sink or Basin, which is part of the vast watershed of the Colorado River.

Critical factors in determining the types of plant and animal life that prevail in different parts of a mountain range are the maximum and minimum temperature extremes. These, along with the mean annual temperature, play an important part in weather conditions as well. Mean annual temperature can be shown conveniently by use of the isotherm—a curving line on a map that indicates the series of points along the ridges and meadows where the average year-round temperature is forty degrees or fifty or sixty. The mean annual temperature is as important as latitude or altitude to life and activity in the mountains.

Timberline in a mountain range generally follows the fifty-degree isotherm; in the Sierra, this is higher than in most ranges. Wet winds from the Pacific keep the

The vistas of peaks towering beyond great peaks strike the eye with an impact that drains the mind of everything except awe.

fifty-degree isotherm between 9,000 and 10,000 feet, though in exposed areas, peaks and ridges regularly swept by ice-blasts, timberline may drop to 8,000 or 8,500 feet. In the foothills, the seventy-degree isotherm determines the point at which the pine forest begins. Below this line, the conifers survive but do not flourish. On both Sierra slopes the seventy-degree isotherm holds between 4,500 and 5,500 feet of altitude.

In its shallow basin, the lake lies between the sixty- and sixty-five-degree isotherms, but this does not mean that the temperature on its shores never goes below sixty or above sixty-five degrees; isotherms are expressions of average or mean annual temperatures. From September until May, lows of twenty to forty below zero are commonplace around the lake, and on rare occasions a night of howling wind pulls the temperature down to minus eighty or ninety degrees. Coming suddenly, as they most often do, such blasts instantly freeze the sap that remains in pine branches. Expanding as it freezes, the sap bursts the life cells inside the branches and fractures twigs and needles. Trees hit thusly seldom survive; after a hard winter whole lines of browned firs and pines are encountered in the wind-swept areas.

Such extremely cold nights are infrequent. Extremes in most winters range from ten below at night to twenty or thirty degrees above at midday. Summer nights usually bottom out at around thirty-five degrees, and noon highs on summer days will reach seventy to seventy-five; there are always a few forty-degree nights and some eighty- or eighty-five-degree days. But each summer will bring a few nights when the temperature drops down low enough to freeze a respectably thick coating of ice along the edges of any snowponds that remain in the vicinity, though the lake's living water will seldom be filmed.

Glaciers formed the oval-shaped bed of the lake. Most of the 1,500 to 1,600 named and unnamed lakes in the Sierra lie in hollows scooped out of granite bedrock by glacial movement and pressure, though some lake beds are the craters of long-extinct volcanoes. A majority of lakes in glacial beds are shallow; the deepest is seldom more than forty feet, and most of them are twenty feet or less in depth. Volcanic-crater lakes may be very deep indeed, eighty feet or even more. The bottoms of glacial lakes slope gradually, like saucers, while those formed on ancient volcanic cones more nearly resemble a cup in their bottom formation. No matter how asymmetrical they may seem at first glance, these latter are basically circular in outline, while glacial-bed lakes tend to be oval, or long and narrow.

There is a close kinship between our lake and others of like origin and location. It is fed by two surface springs and a small creek; there are probably one or more springs on its bottom that cannot be seen. It has no apparent outfall after the snow-melt water runs off at several places around its edge, but this is not uncommon. Many such small lakes have subsurface outfalls, through clefts or invisible fissures or strata of porous rock on their bottoms. The water drains from these as from a bathtub and replenishes the under- ground reservoirs that keep the springs downslope alive.

Only microscopic types of algae can live in the lake's cold water. It is glass-clear, so clean and transparent that trout and pebbles and even aquatic insects on its bottom can be seen easily at its greatest depth. Its upper layer, the epilimnion, is rarely more than a foot deep and in summer will vary only fractionally from a uniform forty-four degrees. The temperature of the central layer, the thermocline, averages forty-one degrees, and the bottom layer, the hypolimnion, is thirty-eight degrees throughout the summer season. This is warmer than the surface springs, which bubble from the ground at thirty-six degrees, but colder than the creek, which will be heated by sunshine to forty-three or forty-four degrees during its midsummer low-water days.

Even if the lake's temperature invited swimming, there are no sandy beaches around it to invite bathers to walk its shore or children to build sand castles or sun worshippers to spread blankets. Pines come almost to the water along its northern and western shores, although there is a strip of meadowgrass of varying width that divides lake from forest. On the opposite side low broken granite bluffs predominate, not huge and imposing, but scaled to the lake's own modest proportions, fifteen to twenty feet high. Two of these bluffs protrude into the water, the others are back from shore. Between the granite outcrops and the water's edge an isolated pine or two stands amid a growth of juniper and manzanita bushes.

Both of the springs and the creek enter the lake at the narrow ends of its oval shore line. One spring flows through mucky soft ground where skunk cabbage flourishes, and along its shallows on both sides of the infall grow white-heads, pondweeds, and a few horsetails. The second feeder spring runs over gravel; its water gushes from the ground in the midst of a thick willow clump. The creek rises from a spring among the rocks at the top of the basin's rim and reaches the lake by a bed strewn with big stones, some the size of a man's head. At the creek's mouth and along its lower edges small *Brodiaea* bulbs cluster among the rocks. In early summer the creek bounces white-watered, six to eight feet wide, but when the snow melt no longer swells its volume the flow tames to a gentle smoothness and its width shrinks to a couple of feet.

Around two-thirds of the lake, water meets land at the edge of narrow strips of shingle, a golden mixture of sand and gravel where early in the season trout-fry dart in the shallows. This margin of shingle extends two or three yards into the water and is kept shining by the lapping of breeze-stirred wavelets that wash up and drain back, creating a small gentle undertow that rolls the pebbles amid the sands and keeps both sand and stones scoured clean. Winterfreeze also plays a part in keeping the shingle bright. When ice forms and the lake's level drops, the ground along the shore freezes to a depth of several inches and this inhibits the rooting of most plants.

Beyond the strip of shingle the lake bottom darkens to brown along a well-defined line. This color change marks the beginning of a layer of natural detritus that covers the remainder of the bottom: wind-blown pine needles, leaves from the brush, shreds of dried grass and stalks of winter-killed shore weeds, seeds, dust blown in from the valleys to the west and from the high arid mesas east of the ridges.

Ten yards from shore, where the water is hip-deep, the layer of debris will be as much as a foot deep on the gravelled bed, a sponge-like mass that sends up clouds of fine silt when disturbed by the boot soles of a wading angler.

Where the creek enters the lake it washes away this bottom covering; a long thin triangle of bright sandy gravel marks the path the current takes. The bottom coating is what gives the lake its life, however. In the detritus the larvae of aquatic insects mature and provide food for the trout. The layer offers shelter for the tiny inch-long fry when they hatch. In it they find a haven from the bigger trout, which like all game fish look upon their offspring as food. The slowly decomposing vegetable matter on the bottom also produces microscopic diatoms and algae that provide food for the fry until they grow into fingerlings and are big enough to eat insects. Without that layer of debris the lake would be sterile; mountain lakes which have perfectly clean bottoms do not support life of any sort.

Along the section of shore line where the pines grow, the trees stretch from the water's edge over the rim of the basin, and beyond, where the land flattens slightly before plunging into the first of a series of valleys. Most of the trees on the slope up to the rim are whitebark pines, but there are some Jeffreys among them, and an occasional ponderosa. Now, about a third of them are big trees, first-growth giants, because they were too small to cut when the section around the lake was logged.

Scorned by the loggers then, these trees now have a half-century of growth behind them and their trunks are three to four feet in diameter, their tops jut fifty feet or more into the sky. The rest of the trees are second-growth, saplings that survived the disturbances of logging and seedlings that rooted naturally after the cutting was finished and the loggers long-departed. New saplings and seedlings grow between the trunks of the older trees; some are perfect miniature pines and others are straggling deformed shoots. One in twenty of these will survive to become a mature tree.

At its altitude of 7,500 feet, the lake lies in the middle of the pine belt. After the relatively level land ends at the

At its altitude of 7,500 feet, the lake lies in the middle of the pine belt.

basin's rim and the downslope of the valley side begins, there is a steep drop of a thousand feet in less than a mile. Near its bottom a few white firs and an occasional lonely incense cedar appear; still lower, on the valley floor, pines give way entirely to Douglas firs and white firs, either of which will crowd out pines where the air has more moisture than it does at higher altitudes. Firs dominate the broad floor of the valley and continue to do so along its upslope on the far side, but there in turn the firs surrender to pines, Jeffreys and lodgepoles, as the terrain slants upward again. Along the bed of the little creek that winds along the valley floor there are a few thin stands of aspens.

On the side of the lake basin opposite the trees a mountain meadow begins in a brush field behind the granite bluffs that line the shore. The meadow is long and narrow, tilted up the basin's rise, and beyond it a series of ridges rise steplike, their exposed granite edges cutting in clean horizontal lines above the trees that grow on their level steps.

These flat places support a cross section of the Sierra pine forest. First there are whippy lodgepoles, then the honey-gold boles of ponderosas mingle with white firs. As the ridges mount higher the Jeffreys appear, then striated-bark yellow firs. The highest shelf, just below timberline, holds a stand of silver and whitebark pines. The only Sierran conifers that are not represented here are the almost-vanished sugar pine and the extremely rare bristlecone.

Both the forest clearings and meadows around the lake bear seasonally-changing sprinklings of wildflowers. Lupine blooms early and dies, larkspur replaces it. Black-eyed Susans crowd the rocky slopes, mixed with the burry lavender heads of pennyroyal. In early summer there is sneezeweed and milfoil; later, rabbitbrush shines yellow and pentstemon gleams red in rocky places. Buckbush grows among the pines, and in the shadows gossamer filaments of opened milkweed pods catch the sun's fugitive rays. Where the trees are not too closely spaced there is dogwood. Pale pussypaws nod over broken rocky ground, their fuzzy heads pulling down slender stems.

Where the snowpond holds briefly, early in the season, the wet earth encourages camas; it is edible, but not really tasty. Also edible are tiny garlicky swamp onions that dot the wet meadows, and wild cress from around the springs and the wild mustard that borders the edges of old logging-cuts. In undisturbed earth at the forest's borders a big brain mushroom now and then pushes up overnight; there are white puffballs bulging through meadow grasses and fawn-colored *Pluteus* fungi on the trunks of windfallen trees.

All its surroundings combine to keep the lake living, and what is true of this one small body of water is repeated on a gigantic scale throughout the entire Sierra range. At the lake and around it, though, we can see at close hand the interrelationship of each link in the ecological chain that must be kept intact if the mountains are to remain green and alive with animals and birds and insects. Should any series of events occur that would cause a sharp break in the growth chains sustaining its basin, or that would substantially alter the area's character, the lake would die. It would not be death on nature's pattern, which takes centuries to form and unfold, but a quick and violent ending. Because the lake is integral with its surroundings, these too would perish.

Many factors combine to maintain this one small pinpoint in the high country. The lake's existence depends on the harmonious balance of a half-dozen natural elements: air and water temperature, the volume of water inflow and outfall, the existence of bottom and shore line cover for fish and as a harbor for the insect eggs that grow into larvae; the number of trout spawning and the percentage of spawned eggs that hatch; the ratio of fry surviving; the quantity of wind-borne and snow-borne dirt and debris in relation to water volume—all these form links in the chain that created the lake and keeps it a viable entity.

These are not the only links on which the survival of the basin depends, of course. The lake, pine forest, meadow, granite ridges, valley, creeks, springs, plant life, living creatures, are interdependent. They are inextricably linked in nature's creative chain. The chain itself is mutable; its length connects creation, growth, maturity, death, rebirth. It is a long and complex chain, weaving in zigzags rather than stretching straight, but it encompasses the globe, and in some places its links are already dangerously thin.

My wife and I found the lake quite by accident more than a quarter-century from this writing. We had been camped about fifteen miles away, during a deer season that had brought an unusually large number of hunters into the mountains. We were not novices in the high country even then, for we had spent a half-dozen years getting acquainted with the Sierra, from the Sequoia-Kings Canyon area in the south to Mt. Shasta and Lassen in the north. We had penetrated the range from both east and west, had followed to their ends many of the sketchy roads that then existed and had extended our explorations on foot over many of its trails.

That year, we felt crowded by the hunters. Neither of us

had then or have now any ill feeling toward hunters and hunting; we both hunt and enjoy the sport. That autumn, though, we were very tired and had come to the high country only for quiet and solitude. The Sierra was our antidote for an unusually long, active and uninterrupted period of the business life we then led. After three or four days of heavy traffic had brought several uninvited visitors a day to our campsite, we decided it was time to move.

There were roads and trails in the area we still had not explored. We tried a number of these, and arrived late one afternoon at the dead end of a rutted haul-out logging road that remained from some long-ago cutting. The ruts were blocked by a big pine that had been felled across the road by the departing timber crew, but beyond the pine we could see that the ruts continued, leading in an easy incline up a ridge before they dropped out of sight. On the chance that there might be a stream or spring close by, we clambered over the log and walked up the trail, looking as we went for signs that the area had been used recently.

There were few signs of people and none of them were fresh, but other signs were plentiful enough to answer our unspoken questions. The logging road, really a trace now after decades of disuse, had become a sort of superhighway for animals. In areas where water had stood and drained slowly, leaving a tabletop-smooth surface of fine silt, and on stretches of clayey soil, we saw hardened imprints as clean and sharp as though they had been left for identification. There were passage-marks of deer, badger, coyote, porcupine, fox, marten, marmots, chipmunks, ground squirrels, and the trefoil tracks of many birds. The tracks overlaid and intermingled, and there were no human footprints of recent origin.

We walked on, examining the tracks, skirting small tangled deadfalls, branches torn by winter storms from the tall pines that bordered the path, small saplings knocked over or uprooted by the action of washing rainwater or the weight of heavy wet snow. There were places where the road had washed out completely, exposing expanses of loose stones studded with big boulders. In other places the granite bedrock had been laid bare by rushing snow-melt water and swirling winds.

A few signs left by the loggers still remained. A trained timberman could have judged to within a year or so the time that had elapsed since the cutting took place. We estimated twenty years and learned later that our guess had been too short by half; it had been more than forty years since the area last echoed to the thunk of axes and the whining rasp of saws. The logging had been unusually selective for its day. Only mature trees had been cut, and even where the big pines had stood thickest newer trees had been long enough in growing to reach maturity. The duff underfoot and the brush growing between the pines concealed most of the old scars. There were a few metal objects scattered widely around: part of a sawblade, a length of steel cable, an unidentifiable chunk of metal that may have been part of a stove door or boiler. There were stumps in plenty, though many had been reduced to dust by borers, tree-ants and other insects. Some were hidden by moss or by enormous growths of white and orange fungi growing on their sides and tops.

We dallied along the trail, topped the ridge, and saw water gleaming between pine trunks. Turning aside, we picked our way over dry crackling twigs and slippery dead pine needles until we could see the lake in its entirety, glistening in the late-slanting sunlight in its small basin. The lake was small, so small that at first we thought it to be an oversized snowpond. Then we remembered that the month was September, and that even the biggest snowponds are dry by mid-August. As we stood gazing, a trout broke the water's riffled surface, to give us further assurance that we were looking at a living lake. A jay spoke harshly from a tree behind us, and in the shadows a chickaree scolded angrily. Another trout broke water, rolling, not jumping.

For a long while we stood motionless and silent, listening to the basin's voices. We did not know then that they were sounds we would hear repeated over such a long period of years that they would become as familiar to us as the voices of old friends. We had no idea, then, that we would keep returning to the lake year after year, would see it and the ridges beyond and the valley past the basin in all the moods nature affords: under bright skies and dark, at dawn and noon and sunset and by moonlight, with the water mirror-still, ruffled by light breezes, tossed by the wind of storms.

Nor did we realize what dawned on us much later, and then bit by bit, after repeated visits. Several years passed before we realized that this basin, this lake, the valleys and ridges and meadows around them held in a small space everything that existed elsewhere in the Sierra high country.

Here, we ultimately discovered, the entire panorama of the huge range can be seen, still magnificent, but reduced in scale to proportions that the finite human mind can grasp. In some parts of the Sierra, the vistas of peaks towering beyond great peaks strike the eye with an impact that drains the mind of everything except awe. With emotion ruling the brain, there is no room left for the questioning that leads to exploration and eventually to at least a partial understanding of the massive forces that created the mountains, and of the more subtle forces that keep them living. In places like the lake's basin, infinitely varied yet revealing all the repetitive natural cycles, it is possible to find the intimacy that leads to understanding.

THE
CAMPS

W e made our first camp at the lake the day after our aimless rambling brought us to its basin. We chose a spot at one end of the oval shore line between the creek and one of the springs, far enough from all three water sources to escape the mist that in the high country rises from water during the late night and early morning hours. We were close enough to the spring to draw water for drinking and cooking; to the creek to take water for washing; and to the lake to be able to see most of it while we sat at meals.

Past experience in high country camping had taught us to make a comfortable camp with a minimum of equipment in a place that provided both convenience and protection. At the spot we chose, a stand of small pines stood in a broad-based triangle formed by three first-growth giants. We knew the tall trees would attract the lightning bolts that usually accompany late-summer storms, yet these three giants were far enough from the small pines in the center of the triangle to isolate us from the effects of even the most massive bolts. Four small trees gave us anchor points for our shelter; this was a large square canvas tarpaulin tied by its corners to the trees and draped over a rope stretched through the tarp's center. This long taut middle rope was our ridgepole, it peaked the fly so that the canvas would shed water readily.

We spread a groundcloth at the rear of our shelter and placed our sleeping bags there. Finally, we hung another long and narrow tarp across the open end, attaching it to drop cords sewn to the underside of the main tarp. It hung to the ground, cutting off biting winds or blowing rain. We had found that this method of creating a shelter suited us much better than the tents of that time, which required heavy wooden poles and guy-ropes and stakes. Tents made of lightweight fabrics pitched with a self-supporting framework of light aluminum tubing lay far in the future when we first camped beside the lake.

Our other living arrangements were as simple as our shelter. At one side of the suspended canvas fly we fashioned a wall of loose flat stones on three sides of a shallow fire pit and on the stones put a light metal grill. Suitably isolated from the shelter and the spring, in a waist-high growth of brush, we dug a sanitary slit-trench that would also receive our garbage. Fuel was no problem; enough dry windfelled wood lay under the trees to supply us for a decade or longer.

Camping is a term that varies widely in its interpretation. To some it means backpacking with a minimum, a sleeping bag and rations. To us it meant, and still means, establishing a reasonably comfortable shelter with the simplest of equipment and the least amount of work. To some, it means a "recreational vehicle" complete with flush toilet, kitchen range and refrigerator, innerspring mattress, electric lights and television, often parked bumper to bumper with others like it, in a paved roadside area a dozen yards off a busy freeway.

Almost from the beginning of our camping experience, which began many years before we found the lake, we learned that the simplest camps, those which do not isolate us from our surroundings, give us the greatest pleasure. When we are outdoors our sense of well-being is not tied to objects, but this does not mean that we make a cult of the primitive. At home we enjoy home comforts: soft chairs and a downy bed; thermostatically controlled heat and air conditioning; the convenience of turning knobs or flipping switches or pushing levers to summon up heat for cooking and water for drinking or washing or flushing.

These are nice things to have, and many people still believe they are entitled to conveniences as a right rather than a luxury. Deprived of the need to hew wood, to carry water, to walk to a desired destination, and to plan in advance to secure even the most basic requirements, we as a people have tended to forget that the natural resources providing them are limited. Because facts are unpleasant, we have brushed aside the fact that ultimately we may be required to meet our physical needs by using our own muscles and individual ingenuity.

There is no better way of learning to accept this than by staying for an extended time in places where there are no shields between people and nature. Spending weeks or months under conditions that demand the use of initiative, brains, and muscles to secure both essentials and conveniences brings a sobering understanding of life's harsh realities. All humans need the shock of living for a while in places where the wallet, the checkbook and the credit card have no meaning.

This awareness must be renewed periodically. The way we have chosen to renew ours is by camping at the lake. It is our good fortune that we do not consider this a discipline, but a pleasure. The renewal would be unnecessarily harsh if ours were a true wilderness camp, where we would be forced to maintain a self-sustaining unit. We do not face the need to pack in with us in large quantities all the things that give us reasonable comfort. Although the lake is isolated from even minor streams of travel, it does lie at the end of a road that connects with other roads, and in a long half-day of auto travel we can reach a town, one of the few mountain communities that has survived the boom-or-bust days of gold miners, railroad builders and loggers.

We must plan well, of course. The resupplying trip is not hard, but neither is it a matter of a five-minute drive to the supermarket in the shopping center down the street. If we run short of coffee or salt or flour, there are no neighbors from whom we can borrow. Conversely there are no neighbors to deplete our supplies by borrowing from us.

Nor do we need to worry about unexpected guests dropping in for dinner. Summer mountaineers rarely reach our isolated camp; they prefer the comfort of mountain resorts, and the nearest of these to the lake is almost a hundred miles away. Today's breed of anglers seldom seek lakes the size of ours. Most of them prefer to drive on pavement to one of the big lakes or lowland reservoirs where they can walk a few steps and begin casting. The hunters' incursion is of short duration and cursory, at the time when we are beginning to think of breaking camp. Our summer guest-book, if we kept one, would be signed only three or four times in as

Mountain meadows are unveiled, already green, as pentstemon gleams red in rocky places.

many months, and until the Sierra deer season opens in September, the signatures would be added at infrequent intervals.

Hunters today also prefer to camp close to, often just beside, a passable road, and then confine their hunting to easy two-hour hikes from their parked machines. This works to the advantage of the deer population, and it also relieves us of the fear that a weekend sport will mistake one of us for his legitimate game. Just the same, we wear orange caps and jackets when we go away from camp during the deer season.

It's not a reflection of selfishness that our camp is designed for two, but rather the result of our preference to return to familiar and well-loved places. Most campers enjoy breaking fresh ground each summer. We did, in earlier years, and during those years we shared many camps with friends and acquaintances. In part, our experiences then have made us a bit wary of inviting anyone we do not know extremely well to join us at the lake. We have had the chance to observe at first-hand the often unpredictable effects that a semi-wilderness camp can have on individuals of varying dispositions.

Solid businessmen, accustomed to shrugging off the fluctuations of the stock market and the changing of the wholesale price index take a change in the weather as a personal affront and consider a rainstorm a catastrophe comparable to an earthquake. Those who are abstemious at home look on a secluded campsite, away from community observation, as an opportunity to cut loose; from early morning until bedtime they are only vaguely aware that they are outdoors instead of in a cocktail lounge. The ones who for weeks have looked forward loudly and repetitively to "really roughing it" treat a grease stain on their shirtfront as a tragedy, and find that they prefer a flush toilet to a slit-trench in the brush.

Normally phlegmatic individuals are sent into a state of shock by a bumblebee buzzing near them and visibly fight down the desire to run when they see a deer or porcupine. Strong men who can face down a board of directors without flinching are reduced to quaking jelly by a strange noise in the night. The man who trembles when his employer sees him returning to his desk three minutes late from a coffee break walks serenely up to a mother bear with a new cub, armed only with the conviction that the bear will not harm him if he does not show any fear.

Men and women who are tirelessly efficient at their jobs and diligent in performing home chores ignore the irreducible minimum of work that must be shared in camp if all are to enjoy equal leisure. The man who spurns cleanup or housekeeping chores at home as menial and insulting spends an hour after each meal up to his elbows in greasy dishwater, makes all the beds, brings in all the firewood, and generally embarrasses his fellow campers by overworking.

Any campsite shared by more than two people—and sometimes camps shared by only two—will have at least one chronic complainer and one irrepressible optimist. The former faults the food, the bed, the weather, gets a pebble in his boot on hikes, burns his hand on hot bacon grease while helping to prepare breakfast, and drops his pet pipe in the campfire. The optimist creates irritation by finding a spurious bright side to every mishap, minor or major.

Perhaps the most uncomfortable camping companion is the prisoner of civilization. Usually such prisoners are single-minded executives who have been planning for weeks to be away; presumably they have left behind at their offices instructions covering every possible contingency, but they begin to display symptoms of stress the moment telephone poles are no longer to be seen along the road. Hour by hour their tension increases until the urgency to be in touch with their affairs drives them to cut short by five days the week they had planned to stay.

Equally a prisoner is the person who has been growing more and more emotional about his need to get away from the clamor of town, the smell of exhaust fumes, the bustle of crowds. Once away from them, he can neither relax nor sleep. Birds calling rasp on his nerves, the pine-scented air irritates his nasal passages, the solitude bores him.

At one time or another during our camping years we have encountered prototypes of all these unhappy people, and feel genuine pity for their inability to accept nature and to adapt to change. We recognize in them what we might have become.

On the other hand, we feel no pity for the ersatz camper of the 1960–1970s vintage. These are victims of what could be called the turtle syndrome. Just as a turtle carries a shell to protect it from the unknown, the ersatz camper travels within a shell of a pickup topper or van, a recreation vehicle. Inhabitants of these shells are effectively insulated from coming into contact with any fresh surroundings that might upset them.

Turtle syndrome sufferers seek their own kind. They huddle together with bumpers touching for mutual assurance, and leave their shells as little as possible. They may walk a few yards to visit in another shell, where they can talk of things "at home," play cards or watch television. Snugly insulated, they stay up late and sleep through the early day. They never hear the midnight wailing of a mountain coyote, the dawn tattoo of a woodpecker, or the chatter of chickarees in the pines. Their eyes are adjusted to the bright artificial lights inside their shells; they cannot see the stars. In the high country's thin pure air, where the sky is never a washed-out blue, but a rich, deep velvety purple, the stars are brighter than anywhere else.

We see in the turtle syndrome one of the dangerous manifestations of a society badly awry. Unused muscles and senses atrophy, and we have reached a stage where only a limited number of people work at jobs that require forethought, individual planning, individual decision-making, acceptance of individual responsibility. Production by muscle has become virtually extinct. Machines have replaced muscles on the farm and in industry, and humans are trained only to serve the machines. No matter how complicated a machine might be, no matter how skilfully its controls are handled, the person serving it gets little personal satisfaction out of a job the machine completes. Only when humans face natural forces in nature's terrain are they forced to make hard decisions and perform tasks requiring human muscles.

This is why we have sought the uninhabited places such as the Sierra high country. This is why over the years our camps have become camps for two. For this reason, we found ways to extend our stays at the lake, especially after the realization came that here the Sierra was distilled into a compass small enough for us to understand. Our solitary camps gave us time to walk, look, listen, think, observe.

We learned early the great satisfaction that comes from occupying a camp for more than a weekend or for more than a week. The knowledge that they must soon be returning to civilized ways and places leads most campers to forego the small touches that add to a camp's comfort. It is easier to up-end the spare bucket for a seat and to use a box for a table than it is to search for branches with natural curves which make them suitable for fashioning into chairs, or into a back for a split-log bench. It is faster to upend a box than to drive lengths of sapling into the ground and fasten boards across them to make a table that is the right height for dining, with a top large enough to make meal preparation easy.

When a camp is to be used for an entire summer, it's not important that the summer will be short; the word "entire" has such a nice, semipermanent sound. In an all-summer camp, the camper feels he has time to do many things that make outdoor housekeeping more convenient and pleasant. In his heart, he feels that the camp will go on and on, that the improvements he makes will be lasting ones. This illusion also releases him from the need to hurry. He knows that he can take a few hours to begin building a chair or table and then knock off in time to walk up that distant ridge and find out what lies behind it, or trace to its source a creek that he's noticed on the floor of a nearby valley. The chair or table or whatever it is can be finished tomorrow, or even the next day.

When setting up a short-duration camp, the awareness is all too keen that while the ridge and creek will be there forever, the camper will soon be gone. He knows that he will not live out his life in the camp, knows that however hard he tries to stretch a summer into infinity, the effort must fail. But it satisfies his need to feel settled, and to create something lasting.

Anyone who has camped extensively knows quite well that the improvements made in a campsite will last only a short while. Nature has its own way of reclaiming objects that humans have converted to their own use. Nature is always intransigent to the works of mankind and in ways that are often too subtle for the eye to notice quickly, nature reduces man's work or destroys it. Such dramatic manifestations of natural power as floods, earthquakes or storms are easy to see, but these are sporadic and in a way insignificant when compared to the cumulative effect of tiny continuing forces, irresistible and frequently unrecognized, by which nature asserts dominance over man's handiwork.

Since the first astronaut walked on the moon much has been said and written about the alien environment of outer space. The relentlessness of that environment has been

impressed on us by television broadcasts from the stark surfaces of the moon and Mars. Those from the moon showed
little space-suited figures making painful adjustments to unfamiliar low gravity, carefully lifting booted feet from
yielding sands, balancing precariously while walking over
shifting stones, forcing muscles to adapt themselves to
reduced weight when handling tools and equipment. But we
have become so habituated on our own planet Earth to the
efforts we make daily to maintain ourselves in the alien environment we have ourselves created that we forget or ignore the unpleasant fact that the style of life we have come
to expect as a right is basically alien to nature.

We think of weeds in the lawn as a nuisance, not as a bat-
tlefront in the continuing struggle of man to maintain an environment alien to Earth's nature. Seldom do we consider
that the cycle of nature is for weedy plants to spring up on

*Snowplants send up rose-pale stalks through the melting snow, their
translucent flowers at greatest beauty for a span of only a few hours.*

unused ground, wither and die, and by dying where they grew restore humus and nitrogen to the soil. When we mow a lawn and burn the clippings we are depriving the soil of its natural needs. It does not occur to us, when lawn-maintenance chores exasperate us, that nature is fighting back, trying to reclaim a plot of earth that contributes nothing to natural growth cycles.

We accept high-rise apartments, towering office buildings, endless acres of earth covered with asphalt and concrete, as a convenient method of accommodating great concentrations of people in a small area. Our quite normal human egos rule out our consideration of the thought that by creating these population masses we are dislocating natural cycles that renew the soil, the water and the air. We have created an alien environment, one that during this last part of the twentieth century may have reached proportions that nature will not accept.

We continue to look for ways to strip the Earth of its energy resources more efficiently so that our massive population concentrations can be maintained, but we do not ask ourselves whether nature may not be sending us a message: that when cities grow over-large they violate natural laws to a degree that causes them to self-destruct. We see the big cities beginning to self-destruct on a global scale, but we still search for ways to salvage them without really questioning the wisdom of our searching.

We describe occurrences such as coal-mine explosions, offshore oil spills, the breakup of dams as "disasters." Human ego blinds us. We refuse to see them as nature's way of trying to conserve or to reclaim what man is trying to wrest from the Earth. Mankind has always taken more from the Earth than mankind has restored. We have never taken the trouble to study the alien environment of our own planet and to learn ways to live within it compatibly.

We cannot afford to forget that each lawn, flower bed, garden plot, farm, road, street, building, house, railroad, tunnel, powerline, mine or oil well represents an effort by man to create and sustain himself in an alien environment, even though we call the Earth our home. We grow angry and resentful when nature exercises its dramatic forces or uses its more subtle powers. We are convinced that man's way is right and that man must win. Considering the immense potency of the natural forces still undiscovered, it is surprising that we win as often as we do. We do not always keep what we have won; witness Machu Picchu and Angkor Wat.

At 7,500 feet in the Sierra, on the borderline between human civilization and nature's wilderness, the struggle can be seen close at hand, and its never-ending character brought home. It is not a single pitched battle, but a series of skirmishes on a scale small enough to be seen in the round and clear enough to be comprehended by those who do not close their minds.

Patience is required to see most of these skirmishes, for there are degrees to nature's progress in reclaiming its own, and often these degrees are infinitesimal. The speed with which the reclamation moves seems to be in ratio to the effort expended by man in converting natural materials to his own use.

A length of tree-branch or a sapling cut to be used as a tentpole or table leg will remain in usable form for six to seven years if the bark is allowed to remain intact. If it is peeled, the sapling cracks, warps, and becomes useless in two years. Eventually, the bark will dry and fall off an unpeeled sapling. If this is allowed to happen on nature's time schedule, the wood will stay stout and straight; a protective glaze has been forming under the bark while it is drying, and when the bark falls off the glaze preserves the bare wood. If this glaze is scraped away or cut into, then the wood starts to behave as it would have if the bark had been peeled.

A sawed, planed board has a much shorter life than do either unpeeled saplings or rough-sawn boards. After two years of exposure to the high country's weather, tiny cracks appear on the board's surface. In winter, these fill with water from rain or melting snow; the water freezes and expands, and the board begins to warp. In three years the board is useless, in five it will be split widely. The process is inexorable, though rough-sawn boards endure twice as long as those that have been planed. Lead-based or casein paints such as those used before the age of synthetics began will protect planed boards four or five years, rough-sawn boards for ten or a dozen years before the paint must be renewed. Paints based on synthetic materials will last only a year or two.

Stones resist erosion better, but even they are subject to attack by nature when removed from their original resting places. A stone taken from a stream bed or pulled from the earth in which it lies buried at meadow's edge, and used in a fireplace or to pave an area between table and campfire has a short life. Flat stones crack into pebbles and round ones split into hemispheres, often in a single winter. A dry-wall fireplace, built of stones fitted together carefully without mortar, will endure for perhaps five years before having to be completely rebuilt. In a cycle of two or three seasons, though, big cracks will open in a fireplace that has been mortared, unless the mortar is repointed each year. Water, creeping into crevices and expanding as it freezes, turns hairline cracks into fissures.

In the second or third year of our camps at the lake, we paved a small square area at the edge of the spring with flat stones and made a diversion dam of other stones to flood the paved area with water to a depth of five or six inches. This was our refrigerator, where we put fresh meats, vegetables, and cooked leftovers. Stored in screw-top jars and partially immersed in the cold water that circulated around the jars, the foods stayed fresh almost as long as if they'd been stored in our electric refrigerator at home. No matter how carefully we selected the stones and put them in place, the paved area shifted each winter, some of the stones cracked and broke, and our chilling area had to be rebuilt each year.

Under our canvas fly, the groundcloth where our sleeping bags were unrolled covered an area eight by ten feet. As careful campers have learned to do, we cleared the earth under the groundcloth of rocks and root stubs, which will tear a groundcloth and bruise a bare foot. The clearing process had to be repeated each year, and after we decided we'd be returning regularly we spent a great deal of time one summer trying to make our cleared spot permanent. We grubbed out roots and chopped them off, often as deep as a foot below the surface. We dug up rocks and removed them, levelled the ground and stamped it firm. Each year we stretch our fly between the same trees, and each year we must clear anew the area where our groundcloth is spread. Winter heaves up rocks our digging and grubbing had not uncovered, and roots we'd thought we'd gotten rid of surface again.

Even after we began returning to the lake year after year for longer and longer periods, we realized it could not be a home or even a surrogate home, for during the nine winter months the area is inaccessible and uninhabitable. We did not try to build, then, not even a platform that would be left during the winter in the area covered by our groundcloth. Having noted the way in which nature destroys boards left exposed, we knew that such a platform would be less a convenience than a bother, as it would require constant rebuilding.

After several years we did haul in a sheepherder stove. These stoves are simple, almost primitive. They are sheet-metal boxes, shallow and rectangular, open on the bottom, with grid rods welded at intervals across the open side, a door cut in one end, and a stovepipe flange welded over a circle cut in the top. The stove is placed with its open side over a shallow firepit with one or two sections of stovepipe fitted to the flange to provide draft. When the top is scoured clean it becomes a griddle, or it will accommodate several pots for cooking watery foods such as stews and soups. The grid rods support baking tins, and the oven they provide is very efficient. It heats quickly and evenly, produces excellent bread and biscuits, even pies and cakes. The stove is quite easy to set up, virtually indestructible, and uses little wood.

When we break camp at summer's end we cache the stove and stovepipe sections, together with a small supply of dry wood, in a cleft below a big granite boulder. The stove has always been there when we return. We dread the time, which we fear will come some day as more and more people learn the joy of uninhabited places, when we will come back and find that someone unacquainted with the mountain tradition of respecting unguarded property left by others has taken the stove, or, much worse, has vandalized it. When this happens, we will know the time has come to say good-bye to the lake.

In the meantime, we continue to keep the surroundings we enjoy so much as nearly in their original condition as is possible. We have always buried wastes that will decay, to let the soil reclaim them and be enriched by doing so. We carry away such things as metal foil and plastic wrapping film, which defeat all of nature's effort to recapture them.

Part of the pleasure in returning to natural surroundings is being able to borrow such simple needs as pieces of stone and lengths of wood, and to leave them behind, knowing they belong where they are, that they will return to the earth and remain part of it. This is one of the reasons why we make no effort to build a permanent campsite at the lake with boards and mortar, paint and hardware; this is why we are careful to leave no visible reminders of our stays. We know that we are only borrowing the small bits of materials we use, and that they will not be removed from their places in the natural cycles of growth, the destruction which is reclamation.

We have no superstitious feeling that by leaving our surroundings clean and restoring to the Earth what the Earth has loaned us we are propitiating any of the forest deities imagined by our primitive ancestors. We are simply trying to be the kind of guests that an appreciative host or hostess would invite to return.

We understand that we are not pioneers, camping in an unexplored, untamed, unpeopled wilderness, and do not pretend to be, even to ourselves. We do realize, however, just how thinly-populated and little-travelled the area around the lake remains, even in the last quarter of the twentieth century. Since we began our summer camps there have been two airplane crashes within five or six crow line miles of the lake's basin. All the normal aftermeasures were followed in both cases: extended ground searches, air searches, low-altitude scanning by helicopters of the lost planes' known courses. Yet, seven years passed before the remains of one wrecked plane was discovered, and nine years went by before the wreckage of the second was found.

So, though our camp is not totally isolated, it is removed far enough from the civilized routines that are normal to most of us to give us a sense of what the unspoiled wilderness must have been like.

A THE NIMALS

Snow melt begins early in the high country around the lake, but many days pass before the melting is total. It starts on the granite ledges and ridges that rise beyond the basin. The rims of rock, thinly-covered and sometimes exposed, absorb the sun's heat even under a snow-covering. They retain the warmth, and the snow-cover comes under attack from above and below at the same time. From these highest rocky spots the snow vanishes quickly, though in deep crevices and under shelved ledges that shield the ground streaks will remain until late August.

On the meadow the melting is slower, and under the pines it is slower still. In the narrow meadow that lies between the basin and granite ledges, the tips of new grass push up through the surface before the snow's crust begins to fall in patches onto the water-covered ground. Around each grass tip a tiny crater forms and the miniscule quantity of heat given off by the scanty sap in the stem melts the crust. Each day the craters grow larger and the protruding grass tips more numerous. The craters merge and the snow sags and at last chunks of its crystallized surface begin to drop away. In many spots only the surface tension of the crust has been holding it up; the snow below it has been absorbed by the melt-water at the grass roots. Once the tension breaks, the crust vanishes overnight, except in a few spots where miniature drifts have formed at rock-bases or brush-roots. Here, the patched snow will remain for a day or two or three.

Water has already begun moving underneath the crust. Some of the melt runs off the meadow's edges, but there is a saucer at its center, and most of the melt-water flows inward. It collects in the depressed section at one side of the meadow, forming a snowpond that shrinks perceptibly as warm week follows warm week. The pond remains, if only as a green spot, when the rest of the meadow has turned yellow near summer's end. The ground under the still-green area stays soft and even a bit mucky until it freezes hard during the first really cold nights.

Under the trees the melting process is very slow indeed, especially on the western sides of the big-boled first-growth pines. Shaded through the day, the snow here must be melted by the warm air that strikes it only briefly during daytime hours. Craters form around the boles of trees as the warmth of rising sap penetrates through their thick bark, but this heat is not great enough to have any effect at the distance of a few inches from the trunks. Water collects on the forest floor under the layer of duff that has been built up by needles falling, by pinecone cores the chickarees have stripped of their seeds, by shed twigs and shreds of bark, and by a sifting of exceedingly fine airborne dust.

Great isolated snow drifts piled up by winter's whirling winds are the slowest to melt. The winds that created the drifts follow no set patterns. Although in some places the drifts rise predictably, year after year, there are many spots that will hold deep drifts one winter's end and be bare the next. Nor are the drifts predictable as to size or form. A drift may stretch for fifty yards along the edge of a meadow, slanting up in a smooth unbroken sweep until it touches the bottom branches of the trees. A short distance away another drift, sculpted by the wind into peaks or minaret-like towers or dome-topped pillars, may extend into the meadow and leave bare a strip between meadow and forest. One bank of a stream may be drifted high, the opposite bank almost bare. A drift may hide a clump of willows taller than a man's head and ten yards away a second willow clump will retain nothing more than a few shredded fingers of snow extending from its roots.

One year of each four or five brings exceptionally wet and heavy snow to the high country. In these years the roads that lead to the lake may be closed by high drifts until late June or mid-July. Because nearly all the back roads of the high country dead-end or lead to nowhere except such seldom-visited spots as the lake, they are not cleared by the snowplows that keep the constantly travelled highways passable. In years of heavy snow, we defer our start for the lake

until July. Once or twice, when we tried to shovel a passage
for our loaded car we found that we were wasting effort on
futile labor, and learned to adapt our plans to nature's cycle
by waiting for the drifts to melt.

Winters of light snowfall are rare in the high country. Perhaps one year in ten the snowpack between the 6,500-foot
and 8,500-foot levels will average less than fifteen feet in
depth. The normal pack at these altitudes is twenty-five feet,
and in years of heavy snow it rises to thirty-five feet, occasionally more. This is also the average depth of the Sierra
snowpack at altitudes above 8,500 feet, and even at heights
above 10,000 feet the depth of the pack does not increase
dramatically but melts much more slowly. We always find
some snow in the lake's basin when we arrive, but it is
usually patchy, and soon vanishes from all but the most
sheltered places.

When we park our loaded car at the big log that blocks the
road to the lake, we can judge at a glance how easy or hard it
will be to carry our gear to the campsite. Many years there
will be stretches of snow extending for a hundred yards between clear areas of the road beyond the log. This snow is
melting by now—rotting is the word used to describe
it—and though it is deep in only a few places, it is very
treacherous. Walking with a heavy load over rotten snow six-
teen to twenty inches deep makes every step a mild adventure. By comparison snowshoeing or skiing on deep fresh
snow is like strolling over pavement.

Rotten snow is crusted, and the crust is deceptive. It is
hard and firm in some spots, mushy-soft in others. It must be
traversed with careful slow steps, keeping one foot planted
in a spot already found to be solid and supporting the body's
weight on the static foot while the other foot is advanced.
Always, before shifting one's weight to the advancing foot,
the crust's stability must be tested. This involves hard
pounding with a bootheel to learn whether the crust will
support the foot. If a few preliminary taps cause the crust to
cave in, then the foot must be set down hard and stamped a
few times to pack the snow solidly beneath it. Even after this
is done, there are times when the forward foot will sink

deeper or will skid when it takes the body's weight. In knee- or thigh-deep drifts, this calls for wild body-twisting and much arm-waving to prevent a clumsy fall.

Rotten snow is too wet to permit the use of skis or snow-shoes; it clings to both and forms ice-clods. Trying to cross such snow on skis or snowshoes is dangerous, for while either will distribute the body's weight over a wider surface area, the surface of rotten snow is so unpredictably treacherous that half of the side of a ski or a major part of a snowshoe may be planted on yielding crust. When this happens, the foot slides; the skid may equally well be back-ward, forward or to the side, and may result in a twisting fall that strains a back muscle, twists and sprains an ankle, or even breaks a leg.

We've learned to hurry slowly when taking the road from our stopping place to the lake. Our first trip is always made without any load in our arms, and we carry branches with which to prod the surface over the deeper drifts. Once we have packed a trail, the going is predictable. Stepping in our earlier footprints, we carry our gear to the campsite. The later trips are always easier than the first, in spite of the loads we are carrying.

We get to the lake most summers early in June. The high country has not awakened completely even then; the snow is still melting, revealing things it had hidden. Always the melt uncovers the carcasses of a few deer that waited until too late to begin migrating and did not reach the valleys where the herd winters. Usually the carcasses are at the edge of a meadow, where habit has led the deer to look for food. Finding none, the animal has headed for the trees, perhaps to seek shelter, perhaps to gnaw a bleak meal of pine needles and bark off the lowest branches. After a winter of unusually heavy snow there is always evidence fifteen or twenty feet above the bare ground that deer have chewed needles and bark off the branches they could reach. Deep snow is an enemy of deer. Unless it has a thick crust, their sharp hooves cut through and the deer flounder in the soft wet snow below the crust, but cannot escape. They are held captive until they starve.

Carcasses of other animals besides deer are revealed by the melting snow. There are twisted bodies of rabbits and ground squirrels that were hurt by an attacking predator. Even though they escaped, their strength was so depleted that they were unable to reach the safety of their nests or burrows. There are the stiff forms of birds that have misjudged the season and waited until too late to fly south or have returned too early and gotten caught by a late storm. We think of animals' instincts as being infallible, but they are not.

Other things appear as well during the melt's progress. At the foot of a bluff a pile of jackstrawed timbers marks an abandoned mining claim. In a meadow a heap of boards stands where the snow's weight caused a cabin to collapse. Beside a road or trail almost obliterated by time the skeleton of a wagon that broke down and was left to fall apart skews

The instincts of the animals are not infallible, as the stiff form of a bird which misjudged the season attests.

crazily from the uncovered soil. Around old logging stands there are always lengths of rusted, twisted wire cable and shards of metal. In areas frequented by people, the melt uncovers their unsightly discards: cans and plastic wrappings and metal foil and bottles that the slobs among them have tossed aside.

Each day the patches of snow grow smaller and there are more signs that the birds and animals are resuming their summer lives. Weeks earlier the deer began their upslope migration from the foothills and valleys. They move more slowly returning than they did when they left, for some of the does are bulging with the fawns they will drop after reaching their summer high-country range and a few early-born fawns move with the herds. It is difficult to distinguish between buck and doe at this season, for not all the bucks have begun to sprout their returning antlers. The mature bucks are in velvet, but the young ones have only tiny knobs on their heads where antlers are just beginning to emerge.

With the deer come the mountain lions and bobcats that have followed the herd to lower altitudes. A few of the big cats stay in the high country throughout the winter, but the deer herd is the big cats' commissary and most of them follow it to the valleys, living in the foothills, dropping to the grasslands to forage, and now returning to their true homes among the rocky ledges above 8,000 feet. The bear are already afoot. Their hibernation ended before the snow stopped, and they came out of their caves still drowsy, with patched frowsty coats, their grumbling bellies driving them to begin their summertime rambling.

Chipmunks and ground squirrels and chickarees no longer visit their food caches, though usually these storehouses still hold a supply of seeds. The small creatures leave their young in the burrows where they were born during the winter, and scurry to the thawed meadows to refresh appetites jaded by a diet of long-stored victuals. They feast on fresh juicy buds, soft new seeds, and the tart hard berries just beginning to form on currant bushes. Marmots and badgers leave their hibernation and come gaunt-flanked from earthen dens to search for food: sweet fresh grass for the marmots, newly active small animals for the badgers.

Ice creaks on the beaver ponds, then breaks and melts. The beaver ripple the placid water in broad vees as they head ashore to strip willows and aspens of bark in which sweet fresh sap is just beginning to rise. The drone of insects begins to be heard, and the chirps of just-arrived birds. Soon, as the streams and lakes warm, the trout will stir and start to feed avidly, their winter-slowed metabolism responding to the new season.

Through the lengthening hours of twilight and dawn the hooting of owls sounds as they make up for scanty winter hunting, when so few small animals were abroad. Hawks swoop over the meadows, eyeing the ground closely. Grouse zoom from brush patch to brush patch on the slopes; woodpeckers beat the drumrolls of advancing summer as they pierce the bark of trees with their chisel-bills, seeking the new hatch of beetles. The migrants begin to return: robins, jays, painted quail, grackles, mountain bluebirds, chickadees, wrens, tits, sparrows, hummingbirds.

At this time of the year, every patch of ground is soft, often muddy, and bare areas retain the pawprints of all animals. Even the tiniest birds sink deeply enough to leave traces of their claws. It is easy to read the story of their activities. After the snow-water has evaporated or sunk into the soil, decipherable tracks will be found only on abandoned roads and logging trails or in water-softened sandy margins of lakes and streams. In the duff on the forest floor or on bare rocky soil, tracks do not hold their shape well, but show only as smudges.

Even a suitably sandy area of powdery ground will tell more easily read stories of the animals and birds if it is smoothed from time to time with a bushy branch. This prepares a marvelous matrix on which fresh tracks will stand out. The prints left in such prepared areas are etched cleanly. Even when print overlays print, the order in which the animals passed can be determined, and often the record of their movements can be interpreted to give a hint of where the creatures were going and why.

Reading tracks admittedly is not as satisfactory as watching the animals themselves, but tracks are valuable supplements. Because the wildlife around the lake encounters humans only infrequently, the animals and birds seldom hurry to cover at first sight of a person. They are not unafraid or incautious, but neither are they over-timid or as wary of people as are those in habited areas. On seeing an intruder, most of the animals stop what they are doing and freeze into motionlessness, staring at the stranger. If the stranger also stops and remains equally motionless, trading stare for stare, the chances are good that the animal will go about its business—usually, eating—satisfied or accepting the fact that inasmuch as the stranger has made no overt moves, he is unlikely to make any.

Some animals are timid, though, and the only way to learn about them is to use their tracks as a guide to finding the routes they favor and wait in semiconcealment for them to appear. The most rewarding times for doing this are in the very early morning, from false dawn until an hour after sunrise, and in the late afternoon, between twilight and full dark.

Many animals of the high country—chipmunks, ground squirrels, chickarees, marmots and porcupines are notable exceptions—go out chiefly at night. The nocturnals usually begin moving when the sunlight starts to fail, and most continue their prowlings until daybreak. They will be seen for the most part as silhouettes against a fading or growing brightness, or will be sensed rather than seen, the only sign of their presence being an almost inaudible occasional sound or the slightest flicker of movement. On the soft wet earth during snow melt, or later on dusty soil brushed smooth, their pawprints can be read at any time of the day.

Hardest of the prints to tell apart are those left by the smallest animals: chipmunks, chickarees, ground squirrels, woodrats and voles. All these have paws that are quite similar in size and shape, all of them weigh so little that their tracks are very faint, and all habitually move so quickly that even these faint tracks are blurry. Also quite similar and of a size are the prints of skunks, marmots and martens.

Identifying tracks of small animals become easier after observing their characteristic styles of moving. Chipmunks
push themselves with their hindpaws; their forefeet touch
the ground only lightly. Ground squirrels and woodrats leave
clear tracks of all four feet; they walk rather than advancing
in jumps. Ground squirrels have long claws on their
forepaws, while woodrats have short-clawed forepaws and
long-clawed hindpaws. Squirrels are leapers, and the depth
of their hindpaw prints sets them apart from chickarees,
which bound on all four paws, touching the ground
alternately with both front paws then with both hindpaws.

Weasels bound four-footed, too, but they stretch their
long thin bodies when they move, while chickarees arc
theirs. The prints of a weasel will be widely apart, those of a
chickaree closely spaced. Skunks saunter with the rolling gait
of a land-bound sailor; their pawprints are close together on
a center line and often overlap. Martens and minks pace,
their strides even, and leave uniformly spaced pawprints behind them.

Prints of the yellow-bellied marmot, often called a woodchuck, can easily be identified by their triple-arched pads.
Beavers have webbed hindpaws and the prints of their
forepaws show widely spaced toes. The fur-smudged prints
of martens and fishers are much the same shape, but those of
the fishers are bigger and farther apart. Size also distinguishes the prints of foxes from those of coyotes. The
coyotes' paws are much larger, and both resemble the tracks
of a dog. The pugmarks of bobcat and mountain lion are also
similar in shape, four toes above a pad, with claw-marks visible only on the prints left by the hindpaws. Like most of
their species, bobcats and mountain lions can retract the
claws of only their front paws.

Oversized claws on a badger's forefeet make these prints
easy to identify. A porcupine's track can always be
recognized by the furrow its thick stubby tail leaves between
its pawprints as it drags along the ground. The hind pawprints of a bear are remarkably like those of a barefoot man
who has neglected to trim his toenails; because of their size,
bear tracks cannot be mistaken for those of any other animal.

Neither can the tracks of deer. They are the easiest of all to spot and identify, as their sharp-edged hooves cut cleanly even into hard soil. Usually the size, depth and spacing of the twin-crescent hooves will reveal whether the animal is a doe or a buck; the buck's stride will almost always be longer and its prints deeper than those of a doe.

Once acquainted with the more commonly seen footprints, it is not difficult to deduce what an animal was doing when the prints were made. As greatly satisfying as reading a well-written passage in a book or story is being able to read the message of hoofprints in the earth, of having them say to you: A doe with her fawn passed here during the night or in the early morning. Later, a buck followed them; in several places his bigger hoofprints are impressed over the small ones of doe or fawn. Here, the doe stopped to let her fawn suckle; this place where her hooves shifted a number of times without moving forward shows she stopped and the fawn's tiny prints are at an angle to those of his mother. The buck grazed in this patch of whitethorn. Something startled him; his deep-pressed hind-hoof prints show that he leaped for cover into the trees. The doe and fawn had left earlier, for their prints show no signs of a leap.

Not all the tracks tell of peacefully moving animals; some mark ambushes, pursuit and death. The track of a woodrat reveals that the animal moved from one grass clump to another, snipping off the succulent heads with their forming seeds. Suddenly the ground is scuffed and the pawmarks of a coyote appear, deeply impressed. Like any spot where an ambush has taken place, the trails are confused, the earth an area of blurred smudges. But there is enough evidence to backtrack the coyote and find where it waited, crouching, for the rat to come within range of its sudden spring, for the deep grooves made by its hindpaws when it launched the fatal leap are clear enough in the soft soil.

Friends who have never learned the fullness of outdoor living and accept our fondness for it as a mild aberration sometimes ask us if we aren't bored in camp. The question is generally coupled with a reference to the lack of a daily newspaper, a television or radio set. They are convinced that a summer without the information of the press and the contrived dramas of the tube must be barren. They observe that our days must drag because we are so greatly deprived of news and entertainment.

Just the opposite is true. Away from the frenzy of over-communication, the repetitive unreality of stereotyped dramatic characters, it is possible to live in almost complete relaxation. We let time go its own way at its own pace without being reminded each half hour how slowly or swiftly it is passing. We always take a few books with us to camp, but the truth is that we seldom find time to read them. There is too much to be read in the earth and trees and skies. The dramas re-enacted in our minds from pawprints in the soil are real, not invented and acted out, and each is an original, not a rerun.

No stunt man in his rehearsed and planned performance can match the agility and daring of a chipmunk atop a pine tree, or a chickaree launching itself in a soaring jump between branches of trees thirty feet above our heads. No makeup artist can create a countenance as unconsciously humorous as the old-man-with-bad-bifocals face of a marmot. Few orchestras can match the melodies of breezes in the pine forest; no perfume is as subtle as that from a field of mountain larkspur, no singer as melodious as a thrush or warbler at dawn.

As for news of human affairs, by the time the events are reported they have already happened, and there is nothing anybody can do, listening to the report, to change them.

F̲THE̲ISH & INSECTS

Almost every morning during the half hour on either side of sunrise and every evening from an hour before sunset until long after deepening twilight ends visibility, a hundred rings made by rising trout can be counted on the surface of the lake. These are the hours when the fish spread out from the four or five regular feeding stations where they rise in small numbers at virtually all hours of the day.

Most lakes have such regular feeding areas, which anglers hopefully name hotspots. The areas are established by any of several conditions working singly or in combination. One may be created by a prevailing wind current that strews insects from the trees over the water's surface, another by the character of the lake bottom, places where underwater rocks and vegetation provide unusually favorable lodging for aquatic grubs and larvae. A hotspot may be formed by an underwater spring welling up from the bottom and carrying up an almost invisible cloud of silt loaded with the diatoms that attract fry, which in turn draw bigger trout to the spot to feast on the fry. An inlet is almost always a feeding station for small trout that hang in its current to scoop up nymphs or insects washed into the lake by the flow. Experienced anglers work around a lake until they locate these feeding areas, and they will then take fish on days when their less discerning fellows cast vainly to unproductive spots and complain that their luck is terrible.

Although day in and day out the trout feed in their regular stations and move out of them only at morning and evening, there is one night late in June when the fish indulge in a period of unparalleled activity. The phenomenon is not confined to this one lake. There are perhaps fifteen or twenty others in the high country where this night of trout wildness has been observed, and at a guess there are probably twice that number of high country lakes inaccessible to observers until after the key night in late June has passed. The night

Trout-fry dart in the shallows where the water meets the land at the edge of the golden shingle.

when the trout go wild is not on the same date each year, nor does it occur on the same night in all the lakes where it has been observed; there may be as much as three days' variance between the night in different lakes.

There are three Sierra lakes in which I've watched the trout go wild in widely separated years, and over a long period of time other fishermen with whom I've compared notes have agreed with the foregoing conclusions. We have all found that there is no calendar cycle common to all lakes where the phenomenon occurs, that no way has yet been found to determine in advance what night the fish will choose for their orgy of action, and none of us has discovered why the fish go crazy. The only common denominator is that in all lakes, the night occurs during the third week in June.

No one who has seen this phenomenon of nature can ever forget it. The water will be calm, windless, the lake's surface completely flat. No ripples of feeding fish will have disturbed the water for several hours, usually since midafternoon. Then, as the last glow of sunset fades, the frenzied activity begins as though on signal. As the light dies the surface of the water becomes a dark tarnished-silver hue, approaching black. Suddenly, the fish begin to break water everywhere. Over shallows and depths the entire surface of the lake springs to life. The rings of trout rising appear so close together that the usual rippling circles never get a chance to form, but are broken by other circles close by, six inches, a foot away. The lake's calm is totally shattered, its surface is a patternless confusion of crisscrossing ripples.

Very rarely does a fish clear the water with a clean flashing leap such as is made by a surface-feeding trout. Most of the fish are tailing, arcing in swirls just below the surface, breaking the water with only their dorsal fins and tails. The activity may last as short a time as an hour, or it may continue far into the night. Then, as abruptly as it began, the orgy stops. The surface of the lake grows calm and smooth. On the following day the trout go back to their accustomed feeding patterns and otherwise resume their normal habits.

Neither anglers nor ichthyologists seem able to pinpoint any special natural food, such as a subsurface nymph hatch, that would inspire this frenzied action by the fish. A number of fishermen, among them myself, have sampled the water of one or more lakes during this night of unparalleled activity, using fine-mesh dip nets. None of us has found any food that was not in the water the night before or the night after the frenzy occurred. We theorized at first that food must be the explanation, perhaps some translucent organism like the fairy shrimp that are found in some Sierra lakes. The theory did not hold up. Not all the four lakes we managed to sample held exactly the same kinds of subsurface food, though there were some foods common to all of them.

Strangely, ichthyologists have shown little interest in the occurrence, and a few have denied that it could ever happen. Those who accepted fishermen's reports regarding the feeding orgy shrugged off the orgy as an angler's yarn or attributed our lack of success in discovering its cause to the fact that none of us had academic training in ichthyology. One or two of the professionals consulted explained that because a solution of the mystery would not enlarge their knowledge of trout or fish in general there was no reason to seek it. These added that in any event it would be impossible to station enough scientifically qualified observers at enough lakes during the period when the phenomenon could be expected to take place. The matter has actually been pursued with more interest by anglers than by the scientists because of a corollary phenomenon: during this night, none of the dozen or more fishermen with whom I discussed the event have been able to get a strike on any fly, nymph, lure or bait they offered.

This is what makes the phenomenon unique. Many streams and lakes support larvae that hatch at the same time, or are visited by flying insects that swarm over the water, dipping down to the surface to deposit their eggs on it. During a Mayfly hatch trout feed like berserkers, but at such times the angler who matches the natural insect with an artificial fly is almost assured of a good catch. When there is such a generous supply of food available, the trout tend to grow careless or greedy. They strike with an abandon that is foreign to their usual habit of carefully inspecting food morsels and taking them on the jaws only lightly at first.

Lacking clear-cut proof that the night of trout activity is the result of feeding, only one reasonably solid explanation of their behavior is possible. It is only my own theory and has no foundation in scientific research.

Lakes everywhere contain three water-temperature layers, a warm top layer called the epilimnion, a thick central layer called the thermocline, and a cold bottom layer, the hypolimnion. When the seasons change, these layers shift, and the lake is said to "turn over." In warm-water lakes the temperatures of the three layers vary substantially, in high-country lakes the difference is more subtle. Only the few big, deep lakes show marked differences between the layers.

It seems logical that the wild behavior of the trout in high-country lakes where this one-night-in-June phenomenon has been observed might be caused by this turning over of the water layers. Fish are very sensitive to changes in their environment, and may simply be reacting to the turnover of the lakes, much as a herd of cattle will stampede at some sudden change in their surroundings. If food is ruled out as a cause of the phenomenon, this is the only reason that makes sense.

We harvest only a few trout each summer from the lake, a half-dozen a week. Though we fish almost every day, our angling is for the sport of matching our skill against the trout's instincts, and we release many more than we keep. While the fish in the lake qualify as "wild trout," inasmuch as they spawn naturally and are not planted regularly, it's certain that at some time in the past the lake was seed-stocked with hatchery trout. Quite probably the first plantings were made during the 1920s and other plantings in the 1930s, as the lake's fish population is about equally divided between rainbows and browns.

These dates coincide with the changed practices of the state's fish and game department. Browns were the most common trout planted in the 1920s; in the 1930s the emphasis switched to rainbows. Later, during the 1950s, mixed plantings were made of rainbow, brown, brook and cutthroat trout. Because the lake holds none of the latter two species, it's safe to assume that it last received hatchery fish no later than the 1930s.

There are very few high-country lakes that hold native trout. The rainbow is not native to this area, and of course the brown is an import from Europe. In all my fishing of high-country lakes and streams, only three or four natives have taken my fly or bait. The native trout, which locally are called "Tahoe trout," have the plain monochromatic markings of lake trout, although in these smaller trout the reticulations are very faint and appear more as spots than wavy lines, and the fish bear a few dark spots. They are quite similar to the "speckled trout" recorded in other areas of North America by early writers on angling.

Golden trout are the genuinely native species of the Sierra, but they are not found anywhere in the high country. They are the trout of the High Sierra. The species will neither spawn nor survive long in waters below 8,500– 9,000 feet. The original habitat of the golden trout was the Kern River watershed of the southern Sierra, but they are now much more widely distributed in lakes of the upper altitudes.

In about half the Sierra's lakes, trout will live but will not reproduce. Most of these lakes lack suitable spawning areas, and trout are among the most demanding of all fish in their egg-laying requirements. These are very specific: clean beds of gravel, aerated by current or water movement, within a temperature range of forty-eight degrees to fifty-three degrees Fahrenheit. Our lake meets all these requirements, with its creek inlet and edges where the water is aerated by wind action, so the trout in it do spawn each year, and the fry have the necessary food to support them while they pass through the fingerling stage and grow to a short maturity.

Many high-country lakes have beds of solid granite, thinly covered by sandy gravel and wind-blown debris, but have no aerated spawning zones, nor do they have enough food to support trout fry. A substantial number of high-country lakes stay replenished only by snow-melt water, others have sheer rock borders that drop abruptly to bottom around much of their perimeters. Winterkill is rare in the high country, but is commonplace above timberline. Most lakes in the 8,-500-plus altitudes are quite shallow, lying in glacial gouges, and during the long winter become almost solid blocks of ice. It is in lakes such as these that trout are winterkilled.

Many fishermen believe that winterkill is caused by anoxemia, lack of oxygen, but this is not the case. Even in shallow lakes covered by a thick ice layer and piled high with snow-drifts atop the ice, trout can extract from the water all the oxygen they require. They can also survive through an almost foodless winter, for like all wild creatures, trout can survive extended periods of starvation or semistarvation.

They cannot, however, withstand the metabolic changes that take place in their bodies when the temperature of the water they inhabit drops below thirty-six degrees and stays at or below that point for a week or longer. At thirty-six degrees a trout's metabolism is arrested. It becomes unable to digest food, and whatever is in its stomach or is taken into its stomach decays, poisons the fish, and kills it, no matter how much or how little oxygen the water holds.

In small high-altitude lakes a trout's life span is short and its growth limited, and these lakes must be stocked on a three- to four-year cycle to maintain a trout population in them. Fish in warmer, food-rich lakes at lower altitudes grow throughout their lives, which vary according to the species. Rainbow and brook trout may live as long as ten years, browns have double that life span. Four years is a long life for any trout in lakes that lie above 8,500 feet, for the food supply in most of them is very scanty.

Even in high-country lakes the size of ours, the fish virtually stop growing after they are four years old. By this time a rainbow will weigh between 1½ and 2 pounds, a brown as much as 3 pounds. It's just as well that the lake holds no very big fish. Like all game fish, trout are cannibals, and the bigger a trout gets the more urgent becomes its need to feed well and often. The presence of even a few very big trout would upset the lake's ecological balance even more quickly than would an army of anglers lining its banks daily.

Fish taken by this mythical army would vary in size in ratio to the entire trout population; there would be small, medium-sized and large fish, and there would always remain in the lake some fish of all sizes that had escaped the fishermen. However, given the presence of even a few big cannibals in the lake, the situation would change dramatically. The big fish would concentrate on the fry and fingerlings, and would within a very few years reduce the spawning stock to the point of extinction. The process would accelerate as small fish became less numerous. Finally a year would come when the cannibals devoured all the fish smaller than they were. A few years later, when the big cannibals came to the end of their life spans, there would be no more trout in the lake. It would revert to its original fishless state.

We harvest our half-dozen fish a week, then, and avoid the curse of the skillet when we cook them. Trout are naturally fat, and some of the oils and fats used in cooking are not compatible with the fat on the fish, while skillet cooking hardens and toughens their delicate flesh. We reserve a small grill for trout and cook them very briefly over orange-red coals, then dust them lightly in the cavities with salt and pepper, and season them with a few drops of lemon juice after removing their skins on our plates. All this is done within a quarter-hour after the fish come out of the lake's chilly water.

Meals eaten beside an open cooking fire, whether the main course is freshly taken trout or another favorite food, are among the great pleasures of camping. However, at the lake and at camps in most of the high country until the first week in July, outdoor eating must be confined to breakfast eaten before full daylight and dinner eaten after sundown, if the meal is to be enjoyed. June is the month when snow mosquitoes rise in swarms from the mountain meadows during daylight hours.

This tiny specimen of the *Culicidae* is the only really pesty insect found in the entire span of the high country. Below the snow line, at 5,500 feet, insects of all kinds are plentiful, as are snakes and lizards. At 6,000 feet the snakes vanish, except for a few harmless water snakes, and insects thin out both in numbers and in variety. Above 7,000 feet only a few innocuous insects will be encountered, and there are no snakes of any kind.

In the high country proper there are forest spiders, most of them tree dwellers, which spin small untidy webs across deserted woodpecker holes and in branch crotches. At meadow edges a few orb-weavers construct large webs in perfectly concentric strands. Wolf spiders and jumping spiders spin no webs at all, but lie in ambush among the meadow grass roots or on tree trunks and leap out on other insects. Few of the spiders bite humans; on the rare oc-

casions when they do, the poison is so harmless that it raises
no welts.

There are no wood ticks in the high country to attach
themselves to animals or humans, no chiggers, no fleas. The
few other insects in addition to the spiders are wood borers
and beetles, termites and wood ants. These are interested in
trees, not flesh. They provide food for woodpeckers and
nuthatches and other tree-hopping birds. Their eggs are laid
under a thick layer of bark and develop into grubs that bears
relish greatly. Torn bark on trees, especially deadfalls, is a
certain sign that there are bears in the neighborhood.

Bumblebees drone around patches of wildflowers. Flies,
bluebottles and deerflies, often zoom up into the zone above
6,000 feet. Lacewings and sawflies zip above the meadows
and are snatched in flight by darting flycatchers. From midsummer on, small swarms of gnats cruise low over the lake's
shallows, and there are other flying visitors, chiefly of the

Wood ants lay their eggs under layers of bark, providing grubs for the bears.

mayfly family, that hover over the water to drop their eggs. The eggs sink to the bottom and swell; larvae form inside them and emerge as nymphs that crawl up on stones or the stems of bottom weeds, where trout pick them off. The lake supports a moderate population of water insects: water striders, water boatmen and backswimmers are those most often noticed, as they are surface swimmers. Other aquatic insects are rarely seen because they stay close to the bottom.

Almost all the insects provide food not only for birds and meadow mice and shrews, but for other insects as well. Many, if not most, of the high country's insects and the grubs that come from their eggs are great devourers of decaying vegetation and animal matter; they are the garbage disposals of the Sierra. The only unwanted, unsightly and unnecessary trash they cannot cope with is that deposited by humans: the litter of metal, glass and plastic. None of the insects common to the high country are venomous. A few—deerflies, for instance—will light on and nip exposed human skin, but the bites are more noticeable than painful.

From early June until Midsummer's Day, though, wherever there are wet mountain meadows there are snow mosquitoes in uncountable billions. Unique among their species, snow mosquitoes have a dual reproduction cycle. During the swarming period in June they lay their eggs on water accumulating on the meadows from the snow melt. The eggs float until the water sinks or runs off, and as it drains, the eggs stick to the exposed grass stems. As the grass dries, so do the eggs. They lie dormant under the winter's snow, and not until they are touched by water during the next summer's melt period do the larvae emerge. They wriggle briefly on the water that is now rising in the meadows and hatch in a matter of hours into mosquitoes. Their reward for months spent in a state of suspended development seems inadaquate, for the life of a snow mosquito is measured in hours. They hatch at sunrise, swarm through the daylight hours, mate at some time during their day's flight, and late in the afternoon deposit their eggs. At dusk, they die.

Before the sun comes up and after it goes down there is not a mosquito to be seen anywhere. Campers can sleep undisturbed and unsheltered; there is no need for nets that tangle with sleeping bags during the night. If breakfast is eaten before sunup and dinner deferred until after sundown, both meals can be eaten outdoors without being interrupted by the constant slapping-away at hordes of mosquitoes. A noonday meal can be eaten only on a ridge where the breeze is brisk, or in a net-shielded tent, or in a cabin with closed doors and screened windows, else the eater runs the risk of getting a mouthful of mosquitoes with every bite. Strangely, the mosquitoes do not hover over water; they do not bother an angler in a boat or even one wading a few yards from shore.

These are tiny mosquitoes, only a little bigger than gnats, but their stingers are long and powerful. They will probe through a thick wool shirt and undershirt, so the high-country camper quickly learns to wear two shirts in June, or a jacket of closely woven material over a single shirt. The probes of snow mosquitoes will even go through the tough material of denim jeans and covert cloth trousers, though they are not long enough to penetrate trousers worn over woolen underwear.

Oddly, the sting of one or two snow mosquitoes is seldom painful or even felt, the insects are so tiny that a victim must be bitten by several dozen at the same time and in the same area of skin before feeling any real discomfort. An isolated bite or two or three will itch for a moment, then the pinhead-sized welt raised by the sting subsides and the itching stops. When bitten by a swarm, though, the affected area will puff up and sting and smart for several hours. No salve or lotion seems to be effective in bringing relief.

During the snow mosquito weeks anyone outdoors between sunrise and sunset learns to wear heavy clothing in layers—which the cold air would compel him to do anyhow—and tuck his trousers into his boot tops. One must smear one's hands and face with insect repellent, not overlooking the back of the neck and the forearms, where a strip of skin is exposed by cuff plackets. In this day of effective repellents, snow mosquitoes have become a minor nuisance, and that only because they travel in clouds so thick that when they settle on a person's clothing someone standing ten feet away cannot tell the color of a bright red shirt under the swarm. Except in areas where repellent has been applied, the victim's body is a solid black mass.

After Midsummer's Day, the summer solstice, which falls in the third or fourth week of June, the mosquito season ends. By this time most of the meadows have begun to dry; the snow-melt water has run off or collected into ponds, and the mosquitoes vanish. Their period of activity is proportionately as short as their individual life spans, but on the stalks of meadowgrass they leave behind the eggs that will produce next year's swarms.

Insect life cycles are endlessly fascinating. In some years another high-country insect is almost as numerous as the snow mosquito, though it does not appear with the same metronomic regularity. The insect is the tortoiseshell butter-fly, which drops its eggs on the manzanita brush fields during its late-summer life-span of thirty to forty hours. Tortoiseshell butterflies appear in swarms on unpredictable cycles. Only a few will be seen during a three- or four-year period; then, following a mild winter, the tortoiseshells will swarm by the million over the brush fields. Their numbers will be so great that there will not be room among the manzanita and juniper to accommodate the swarms. The butterflies fan out over the meadows, into forest glades, onto beaches. In years when summer nights are cold, many of the butterflies die before depositing their eggs; in years of exceptionally hard winters, many of the eggs do not form larvae.

An instinct seems to keep the tortoiseshells from going above 8,000 feet. The cutoff line is not knife-sharp; a few stragglers do go above that altitude, but they are numbered by dozens or scores instead of millions, as are the swarms that are encountered between 6,500 and 7,500 feet. The butterflies spread their arrival over a period of several days, and stay only three or four. Yesterday, they hovered with fluttering brown-gold wings over the brush fields and meadows; today they have vanished. Only the litter of their bodies along the lakeshore and on the bare ground proves that they made their visit.

Dragonflies are always with us during the summer. There was a day when we lounged on one of the granite bluffs overlooking the water on one side of the lake. We were lying on our stomachs, our heads extended past the vertical stone wall, watching the trout feeding on the bottom at the granite's base. It was early afternoon, and the sun was not slanted enough to glare on the surface; we could count the grains of sand and pebbles below the trout, twenty feet under water.

A windfallen pine tossed into the lake by some fierce storm of years past slanted from the top of the granite bluff to the bottom of the lake. Its butt was on the bottom and most of its branches had fallen away; its bark had also peeled off and disappeared. The section of the tree above water was weathered to a light grey, and one of the few branches that remained on the upper section of its trunk curved to within a few inches of our heads. Though we were primarily interested in the trout, my eye caught the suggestion of movement on the branch. It was a grub inching along just below the surface of the water, moving so slowly that my first thought was that the slight ripple on the surface of the lake had deceived me into thinking the grub moved.

Slowly, infinitely slowly, the fat cone-shaped amber-hued grub crawled up the branch until it was out of the water, an inch or two above the surface and a yard or less from our eyes. The grub stopped, as a human might after completing a long and tiring journey. At the speed the grub moved and considering the length of the tree trunk it must have traversed if it had begun at or near the lake bottom, its journey had indeed been long and tiring.

Just then a flurry of darting motion by the trout caught our attention. The fish were darting at the base of the weathered tree trunk as though attacking it. We decided that the grub on the branch beside us must have been one of several using the tree as a road to the fresh air, and that the trout were feeding on those still under water. We watched the fish until their activity slacked off, then remembered the grub on the branch and turned to look at it once more.

While we'd been looking at the fish, the grub had moved

closer to us; it was now only a foot or so from our faces. Close up, we could see that it was humping its back as though stretching. While we watched, a thick, hairy cilium burst from the back and lay slackly black and slightly moist along the creature's yellowish body. Peering closely, we could see that a slit had opened to release the cilium. As we watched, the opening widened imperceptibly to release a second cilium, and almost at once a third, followed by a fourth.

Emergence of the third and fourth cilia had caused the slit on the back of the grub's casing to open quite a bit, and through the translucent shell we could see something stirring inside the casing. A bit more movement, and we could make out a dark curved formation under the shell. The curve began to expand, and a loop of it popped free through the slit in the casing. The dark inner body moved, slowly at first, then with greater vigor. When the body began moving the cilia started to change their form. They expanded, grew longer and wider, taking shape bit by bit as two pairs of oblate wings.

Along the front edge of each wing the black lines of the original cilia were drying and shrinking into a thin rim while the wings were expanding into transparent membranes. The sun was shining full upon them, and we could see them dry and become stiff. Soon a fine tracery of lines became visible over their surfaces.

Most of the insect's body was still inside the casing or shell that had housed it as a grub. The body was visible now as a narrow dark shadow, still looped into an almost full circle. Only a section, about a third of the loop, still protruded from the slit shell. The loop began to grow longer and took on a hooklike shape. It started to vibrate rhythmically. The vibrations split the back of the casing for its full length; the shell gaped open to release the emerging insect's thorax and, at the last, a pair of swollen, globate-faceted eyes. Below the eyes a pair of stubby antennae unfolded as though they were hinged, disclosing a rounded snout. Now for the first time the insect was visible in its final form: a dragonfly.

Not all of its body had emerged; a short length of the tail

section was still caught in the shell. The dragonfly did not try to pull the still-encased section free, but remained utterly motionless for three or four minutes. The bright sunlight showed quite plainly that the eyes were still covered by a lucent membrane that had protected their delicate surfaces while they were emerging from the shell. Under the membrane, the faceted formation of the eyes could be seen in dim outline.

After it had rested, the dragonfly began to stir. First its antennae twitched, then the thorax began to sway from side to side, and with that motion the thorax expanded and became round. The long tail flipped free of the shell and extended itself from the thorax in a straight line. Segmented sections started forming on the tail.

Suddenly, in the space of a breath, the film that had covered the eyes dissolved. For the first time their facets caught the sunlight and sparkled like clustered miniature jewels. The birth—or metamorphosis—was complete. The dragonfly rested motionless for another few moments after its eyes had cleared, then began to flick its new shining wings in short tentative motions, as though to test their strength. It rose straight up from its discarded casing, hovered above us for a moment, then darted across the lake and vanished in the dark shadows of the pines.

BTHEIRDS

SIX

SIX

S ummer is still a promise of the future when the non-resident birds begin returning to the high country. Some anticipate the season's change too far in advance, belying the common notion that all animals and birds have some mysterious infallible weather sense or instinct. These bad guessers return to their summer nesting-grounds too soon, are caught in late storms, and do not survive to mate or nest. The melting snow uncovers their small bedraggled bodies, crumpled beside the bases of trees, their eyes filmed, thin claws clinched, once-shining plumage drab and dull.

Most people think birds are fragile and delicate, but they are not. Fragile they may be, with their thin hollow bones and toothpick legs; yet birds are surprisingly tough, and many of them combine with fragility a hardihood which enables them to weather the months of subzero cold and deep snows that winter brings to the Sierra's upper altitudes. These birds become all-year residents of the high country, and survive the unexpected late-season blasts that take toll of the too-early migrants.

A majority of the area's red-tailed hawks remain through the year, though a few move to lower altitudes where food is more plentiful. The few surviving golden eagles that live among the barren High Sierra crags stay in their stick nests on the upper ledges; in winter they drop down the sheer face of the eastern slope on swift far-spanning wings to hunt in the snowless desert country. The great horned owl is another year-round resident; its thick downy feathers protect it from the cold.

Blue grouse stay in their favorite nesting places at the edges of small forest clearings. They have plump, thickly feathered bodies, and a stockinglike fringe of feathers extends down their legs to keep their feet warm while they buzz close to the ground, exploring the currant and manzanita bushes for shrivelled winter-dry berries, or perch on iced pine branches to nip off tender needle-tips. Cassin finches also remain during the snowy months, feeding on dry buds of aspens and willows. Even on the coldest days, as long as the wind is not blustering in a gale, the staccato tapping of woodpeckers echoes through a forest largely silent under the snow. Most of the smaller birds migrate, though the black phoebe and the winter wren remain to brave the chill and are on hand to greet the returning migrators.

Among the earliest to show up are the robins and the Clark nutcrackers, both big and sturdy by bird standards. Both habitually appear long before the snow melt has advanced beyond a token softening of the pack's crust, while the meadows are still covered except for a few bare patches around the edges and along the banks of streams. The robins seek these small uncovered spots and hunt in them intensively, flying from one patch of bare ground to another in an endless seeking round. Robins are ground feeders, they hop over the water-filmed earth in search of grubs and insects. Their feet are wet most of the time, but this does not seem to bother them. The nutcrackers find perches low in the trees at meadowside and swoop out to snap in midair the few insects that fly across the clearings at this early stage of summer.

Following the robins and nutcrackers come the mountain bluebirds, the male gaudy in electric blue, the female a drab grey. They join the robins on bare spots around the meadows, alternating periods of feeding with quick flights into the pines, looking for an abandoned woodpecker hole they can take over for a nest. Tiny mountain chickadees are early arrivals, too. They remain among the trees, pecking into crevices in the bark to garner ants and pine beetles. Like the bluebirds, the chickadees nest in woodpecker holes. They prefer to nest within a few feet of the ground, and will seldom be seen higher than human eye-level in the trees.

Robins are meadow feeders, seeking their insects at the grass roots. Their rosy wings and grey bodies make them easy to identify. Juncos also feed on the ground, both in meadows and forests, but they prefer seeds to insects. Juncos are often mistaken for sparrows; the two are almost the same size, but the junco is darker. Its feathers are solid brown, while sparrows have salt-and-pepper markings. Any nests found at a meadow's edge or a few yards into the trees will more often than not belong to a junco pair.

All but a few of the migratory birds return in their thousands long before the snow is gone. They wing in from the western valleys and snowless eastern mesas where they have wintered. There are few prolonged courtships, such as are commonplace in warmer climates, among the birds seeking to mate. In the high country the birds have no time to observe formalities, the summer season is too brief to waste on lallygagging. The returned birds pair up quickly, and the mated pairs start at once to build their nests.

Almost invariably it is the female's prerogative to choose the nesting site, but her choice is subject to the male's approval, and his is the final word. A few bird species make a joint project of site selection and flutter in pairs from tree to tree or bush to bush in search of a suitable location. Much more often the female makes the search alone. The male shows up only after she has found a well situated branch crotch or a vacated woodpecker hole, and often she has begun the nest before her mate arrives.

If he approves the site, the male goes back to feeding, but if the choice of a location does not please him, the pair engages in a short period of angry chirping that ends with the female deserting the already-begun nest and going to look for another spot. When she finds one, it will as often as not be within a few yards of the site the male has just vetoed; it may be no more distant than a higher or lower branch of the same tree. The male joins her for another inspection, and if he approves her choice the female begins to work once more.

An extremely fortunate bird watcher may on occasion find a location similar to one we stumbled on. It was at the edge of the meadow, upslope from the lake, and a pair of mountain bluebirds, a pair of robins, and a pair of mountain chickadees had all selected nest sites within a five-yard radius. The bluebirds chose an old woodpecker hole in a snag-tree, about fifteen feet above the ground. After several false starts, the male robin finally approved the female's choice of a well-protected crotch in the branches of a whitebark pine, about thirty feet up. The chickadees discovered a woodpecker hole no more than eighteen inches above the roots of a small pine and began building in it.

Morning after morning, beginning just before sunrise, the three mated pairs were busy at their nesting sites. After a period of shyness or caution that lasted for two or three days, all three pairs accepted my presence as a harmless nuisance, and ignored me while going about their construction jobs.

Of the three pairs, the robins were the most suspicious. The male remained close to the female virtually all the time I was close by, flying shotgun when she went in search of suitable twigs and the dry grasses she used to weave them together, and later the moss with which to line the nest. However, when I settled for watching them from a distance, the male paid little attention to his mate. He winged out to the meadow to feed, visiting the nesting place only occasionally to make sure the work was progressing satisfactorily.

Not all the female's time was devoted to working; she took frequent insect breaks, joining the male on the bared areas around the meadow, where both hopped busily in search of food. It took the robins almost two weeks to complete their nest; perhaps the extended time was partly my fault, for whenever I went too close to the tree the pair stayed together, and the female's efficiency in her construction job was slowed accordingly. If they thought me too near for safety, the male convoyed his mate to the tree, she carrying a load of nesting material in her beak. Then he perched on a limb just above the nest-crotch and eyed me suspiciously while keeping the female under observation.

Though the bluebirds were almost as suspicious of my presence as were the robins when I got too near their snag-tree, the male bluebird was not as solicitous of his mate's safety as was the male robin. While the female was busy looking for grass stalks and moss, the male bluebird wheeled over the meadow, his brilliant body glistening in the sunshine and his electric-blue wings whirring as he swooped down on flying insects. Then, when the female had gathered a load of material and started toward the snag-tree, the male veered to join her.

While the female popped into the woodpecker hole to arrange on its bottom the grass or moss she'd picked up, the male stood guard on a stubby branch just below the hole. When the female emerged, he entered the hole, possibly to inspect her work and perhaps to rearrange a strand or two of grass. His inspection ended, the male emerged from the hole and the pair flew off together. They did not stay together, though; the male went back to catching insects, while the female collected a fresh load of material.

Least timid of the three pairs were the mountain chickadees. These are tiny birds, barely three inches long, with dark grey wings and backs, pearl-grey breasts, and heads capped in black. The male chickadee, like the male robin and bluebird, did none of the work connected with building the nest; it was the female that gathered all the materials and arranged them in the tree cavity. Nor did the male chickadee guard its mate as closely as did the bluebird and robin. While the female worked hard, making a fresh trip with moss or grass at intervals of five to ten minutes, the male worked up and down the nest-tree and other trees nearby, searching bark crevices for food. Only occasionally did he enter the nest to inspect and presumably approve what his mate was doing.

My close presence did not bother the chickadees in the least. Now and again, when the female was busy, the male's quest for food brought him to within a yard or less of where I stood, and on such occasions he would do no more than cock an enquiring eye at me before moving on to the next likely-looking bark crevice. The female ignored me too after the first three or four days. Time and again on her trips to and from the nest-hole she would brush by me within inches. Even when I got within a foot or so of the woodpecker hole she continued to pop in and out on her busy rounds. She acted as though there were no strange human within a dozen miles.

Except for grackles and jays, few other birds in the high country are as tolerant of human proximity as are chickadees. Two of my friends from the U. S. Forest Service invited me on a trip they were making to investigate a report that a pair of eagles was nesting on a nearby ridge. As it turned out, the birds were red-tailed hawks that had taken over an eagle's abandoned nest, but that is beside the point. We walked for perhaps eight miles along an 8,500-foot-high ridge, where grouse whirred from brush clumps, deer moved between the pines, and frequent droppings showed that bears had passed by during the late night hours.

We were in a thickly forested area that had not been disturbed by loggers or anglers—water was scarce in the vicinity—or by any except an occasional hunter for almost a half-century. The only human castoff we saw during our hike of almost two hours was the badly rusted flat tobacco tin of a type that had not been used for more than a decade.

When we located the nest in a tall yellow pine and inspected it with binoculars from a distance, a down-breasted fledgling was perched on its rim and the heads of two, perhaps three, others were visible intermittently inside the nest. The nest itself was typical of those made both by eagles and hawks, an untidy shallow construction of small branches and twigs that looked as though they had been joined together willy-nilly, higgledy-piggledy. The fledgling perched on the rim was feathered out enough to convince us it was a young hawk rather than the eagle we'd hoped for; neither of the parent birds was in sight. Because young raptors require frequent feeding, we agreed that the mature birds were hunting and must return soon to feed the chicks.

Carefully, keeping under cover of the close-growing pines, we worked downslope toward the nest. We hurried as much as we dared, hoping to get close enough for photography while the young birds were being fed. We'd seen the nest first while it was almost level with our position on the slope, and as we came closer to it we could see for the first time that the nest-tree was isolated in a clearing, on a flat, with no cover and no slope near enough and high enough to offer much choice of camera positions. We settled for the best we could find, a rise at the edge of the clearing where the trees began to thin out, and hoped they'd hide us from the parent birds.

A quarter-hour passed before one of the hawks returned. We saw it coming in high as it left the cover of a cloud, dropping down swiftly in a direct line for the nest. Our hope that the place we'd selected had enough foliage overhead to hide us was disappointed. While still high, the returning hawk saw us and veered from its flight path with an angry screech. The screech was followed by a series of high-pitched calls, squi-eo, squi-eo, as the parent bird began circling the clearing. The fledgling that had been perched sleepily on the nest's rim vanished inside at the first warning call, and we did not see it or any of the other immature birds again. The parent hawk kept up its soaring, at times dropping almost to tree-top level, and on one swoop perching for a few moments on the very tip of the tallest tree across the clearing from the point where we crouched.

Intermittently, the bird repeated its shrill warning cry, and though we tried to hide behind the trunks of the trees around us, we were obviously very visible to the hawk when it soared overhead. We held our places for perhaps an hour. Noon had passed and the sun was beginning to drop. We could tell by the shadows beginning to creep across the clearing that within another hour or so the trees surrounding the nest would put it into shade that made photography impossible. We listened to the soaring hawk's shrill cries increasing in frequency, and lost hope that it would drop down to the nest as long as we stayed close by. We gave up, and left.

Not all birds are as intolerant as the raptors of people in the vicinity of their nests, but not all birds have been the target of hunters as have the hawks and eagles. Hawks and eagles have not been hunted for food or for sport but simply to exterminate them. Eagles are supposed to swoop down on baby lambs; hawks are by legend the enemies of the farmer's chickens. Neither supposition nor legend stands up to the facts, but both die hard.

While many birds tolerate the presence of humans near their nests, few will allow other birds to encroach on their territory, which may extend for a quarter-mile around the nest itself. The territorial claim of birds is usually asserted against those of the same species or birds of other species that have the same feeding habits. Robins and wrens will chase jays and bluebirds; chickadees, in spite of their small size, will flutter aggressively at much larger woodpeckers. Hawks and owls lay claim to entire meadows, and whether the other birds respect the claims or simply avoid the meadows because they might become food for the hawks or owls is an open question.

Even the tiniest of their kind, the hummingbirds, are zealous in defending an area they have chosen as a feeding spot. These little buzzbombs arrive in the high country late in the summer, usually after the middle of July. They have nested long ago and raised their young in the foothills or valleys where they winter. Hummingbirds follow the maturing flowers upslope; by late July the valley and foothill wildflowers have peaked, but those in the high country are just beginning to produce nectar.

Most common of the hummingbirds in the high country are the iridescent-green annas and the bright pink rufous, the latter the more numerous. Males of both species outnumber females, two or three to one. The hummers settle down in a small territory, usually a clearing sixty to eighty feet in diameter, in which wildflowers are growing luxuriantly, and they are totally without fear in defending their chosen range.

One August afternoon, when my feet grew tired during a long hike, I stopped to rest on an old pine stump in a small forest glade where mountain larkspur was growing thickly. Less than five minutes after I'd settled down, a rufous hummingbird zeroed in on me. It zipped six inches from my nose with the speed and angry buzz of a rifle bullet and returned again and again, now in front, now behind, until I realized that the tiny bird was warning me to leave its domain. Retreating to the edge of the clearing, I found a windfallen pine and sat on its bole to watch the hummingbird hover in front of the opened larkspur blossoms, darting its long bill in to sip their juices.

It fed for ten or fifteen minutes; then a flock of a dozen or so sparrows dropped into the glade. At once the hummingbird attacked, darting at the sparrows repeatedly and scattering them. After dispersing the sparrow-flock, the hummingbird went back to the larkspur until it noticed a ground squirrel crossing the bare earth that bordered the clearing, heading for the grasses that grew sparsely among the flowers. The ground squirrel got the same kind of dive-bombing attack that the hummingbird had launched against me a few minutes earlier. The squirrel retreated even more rapidly than I had.

On the basis of size, the sparrows were three times as big as the hummingbird; they were also a dozen times as numerous. The ground squirrel was six times as big, and I was several hundred times larger in weight and bulk. Yet all of us gave way to the hummingbird's fierce attack.

Jays are probably the best known of the high country's birds, though they are less numerous than others. Their iridescent blue wings and body feathers and their nervous habit of tree hopping makes them easy to spot. A jay will stake out a claim to a camp, especially one where the campers are free with bread scraps and fruit peels, and will glide out of nowhere to chase away another jay or an intruding robin. Most campers are fond of jays. By and large, they are amusing birds, in spite of their habit of serving as volunteer alarm clocks. They seem to consider it the duty of the campers to support them with regular handouts, and if not fed early in the morning take up their position in a nearby tree and scold vociferously until their breakfast is given them. Clark's nutcracker is another bird which shares the jay's camp-visiting habits, though the nutcrackers are fewer in number than the stellar jays of the high country.

Meadow-feeding birds seem to be less jealous of territory than the forest dwellers. Among the meadow-hunting birds, only the hawk consistently chases other feral birds away from a territory it claims. A rich meadow—rich to birds means one swarming with insect life—may be hunted by several species that feed on the wing: dusky flycatchers, Traill flycatchers, swallows, wood peewees, warblers will all hunt over the same meadow without one species challenging or chasing away the others.

Most of the birds that feed on the wing are in constant motion. They dart so erratically, swoop and sweep so unpredictably, that even experienced bird watchers have trouble identifying them while they are feeding. One of the bird watcher's problems is that the birds which take their food in midair are all feathered in shades of grey that vary little among the species. How high they fly is a better clue to identification than color; flycatchers stay close to the grass tops, warblers and peewees range above them, and swallows like to feed at tree-top level or even a bit higher.

Of the forest birds, only woodpeckers seem to have no instinct to stake out a territory and hold it for their own, defending it against other winged intruders. The larger woodpeckers and their close relatives, the sapsuckers, range freely over a very wide area, which may account for their lack of interest in claiming a restricted space. It's not uncommon to observe woodpeckers working the same part of a stand of pines, in trees only a few yards apart, and as though by mutual agreement exchanging trees now and then. The high country hosts a number of woodpecker species, the whiteheaded and the hairy woodpeckers being the most common.

In addition, the smallest member of the tribe, the little black and white downy woodpecker with its saucy red crest is frequently seen among the pines. The downy does not range as widely as its kin. It restricts itself to a territory perhaps five hundred to six hundred yards in radius, and though it does not defend this area against other woodpeckers, it will rarely go beyond its chosen range. Within this distance, there will be perhaps fifteen snag-trees and twice that number of living pines that are in precarious health and as a result are prime targets for borers and bark beetles.

Downy woodpeckers surpass all others of the species in the attention they give to individual trees. They will stay at one tree for as long as a half-hour, exploring each crevice; the bird's tap-tapping bill opens holes just big enough to admit its raspy tongue with the back-slanted barbules that snag and hold the insects as they are pulled out of the wood. A downy will extract as many as ten or a dozen insects from one tree before moving on to the next, and returns to the same trees day after day to be sure it has not missed any of the borers it seeks.

Throughout each day the movements of the little bird can almost be charted by ear, because each tree responds with a slightly different tone or timbre to its bill's tapping. A downy woodpecker is an admirable conservationist, and does something constructive about maintaining natural balances. At the end of a summer it has substantially diminished the number of pine-borers and beetles inside the range it has selected. By reducing the number of timber-damaging insects that lay eggs to grow to the larval stage, the little woodpecker will have given a fresh lease on life to thirty or forty trees. Always, the downy woodpecker leaves its summer home in better condition than it was when the bird arrived.

Not woodpeckers alone, but the entire bird tribe deserves high marks for many reasons. Except for the jays they work diligently in supplying their own needs for food and build their own shelters out of materials that otherwise would be wasted. They live without depleting nature's resources, and simply by living in the high country salvage more ailing conifers than do tree surgeons. They select a territory no larger than is required to care for their own needs, and do not seek to expand it at the expense of others.

Only one bird, the sapsucker, has the potential to damage its environment. While three or four kinds of sapsuckers spend their summers in the Sierra high country, in all there are few of them. The one seen most often is the Williamson sapsucker, a year-round mountain resident which lives at or above the 6,500-foot level. Sapsuckers earned their name because that is exactly what they do: suck the sap from living trees. With short, pointed bills they drill tiny holes in the bark, going in just deep enough to reach the flow of the tree's lifeblood.

They work around a tree in a circular pattern, drilling a hole every inch or two, but always careful not to close the circle of holes they drill around a tree. The sapsucker always leaves an expanse of bark undrilled so the sap's flow will not be cut off completely. If the trees were to be girdled all around, they would die. How the Williamson sapsucker

Spotted sandpipers with their dipping, bobbing walk nest along the shoreline of the lake.

manages to survive the long winter season when no sap is flowing is one of the many unsolved mysteries of the mountains. Presumably, the birds change their diet during the winter and live off the few insects that are available then, or eat pine needles, dried buds or seeds. Their winter rations can at best be marginal; perhaps this is one reason why the birds are so scarce.

Shore birds are almost as common during the Sierra summer as are those that live in the forests and meadows. Around both lakes and streams there are killdeer, spotted sandpipers, black phoebes, and a few water ouzels. All these arrive early, nest early, and leave early. The killdeer or killdee finds a clear spot in a meadow close to a stream bank where it scrapes together a few grass stems for its nest. By the time the eggs have been laid, new grass will have grown up around the nest to hide it. The killdeer and the mountain quail, which is also a meadow-nester, share a common habit. Both lure intruders away from their nest area. The killdeer does this by pretending to be wounded or hurt, dragging a wing and allowing itself to be almost caught until the stranger is out of the nest area; at this point the killdeer whirrs away. The quail may do this too, but often it simply walks away from the intruder, keeping just out of reach, then winging off when the danger to the nesting spot has been averted.

Spotted sandpipers have the same dipping, bobbing walk that is characteristic of the killdeer. It is a sort of nervous hop; its head bobs up and down very much like the small bird-figurines once seen bowing over a container of water in novelty shops. Fishermen encounter spotted sandpipers often, for the bird nests along shore lines and seldom goes far from the water. Another bird seen by anglers, often to their surprise, is the water ouzel. Unique among high-country birds, the ouzel walks underwater along stream beds and close to the margins of lakes, searching for the aquatic insects on which it feeds. It can stay submerged for several minutes, and often bobs out of the water at the feet of a startled angler.

Few water birds are seen in the high country during the

early summer, for when they are moving north the Sierra lakes are still covered with ice and snow. On their return migration the mountain waters are open, and the birds use them as stopovers on their long flights. Ducks of most species, mallard, pintail, redhead, mergansers, and teal, light to rest and usually stay for a few days. Canada geese light on the bigger lakes, and occasionally a pair of late-moving northbound geese or ducks will pass by after the ice has begun to break, and rather than travelling on will stay and raise a brood.

During summer's waning days, the coots—mudhens to most of us—drop in by the thousands on the larger lakes; the smaller ones do not have enough surface area to attract them or enough underwater vegetation to feed them. Grebes, or helldivers as they are more commonly called, are also late-summer visitors, but their numbers are always scanty. Often a flight will consist of only a half-dozen birds, and it is unusual to see more than eight or ten of these bottom feeders on a lake at any one time. The grebes come late and leave when the frosts return night after night. Infrequently during summer's peak a wayward seagull visits one of the high-country lakes and stays for a day or so, but gulls seldom remain long.

Although we are not dedicated bird watchers, we are always aware of the birds around the lake. They serve as our calendar for the summer. We know that the season has officially arrived when we see the first mountain chickadees, that the season has passed its halfway mark when the hummingbirds appear; the presence of water birds is our notice that winter is not far off. We begin to think about packing when the grebes vanish, for while we have come to understand that birds do not have an infallible instinct for seasonal changes, we realize also that their instincts are far better developed than ours.

THE
SHAPING

I n settled places we use street names to identify a specific location, or to guide a stranger seeking to find his way to an unfamiliar place: "Our house is at 234 Ecks Street," "I'll meet you at the corner of Third and Main," or "Wilson's Store is on Birch Street, turn right at the next corner and go about three blocks."

No roads are marked in the high country unless the area is under Forest Service supervision, in which case there are signs posted at turn-offs leading to the chief lakes and landmarks. Lacking markings, one fork looks very like another; one stand of pines cannot be distinguished from the next by a stranger; the small creeks are about of a size; and even the biggest boulders split and shift when snow-melt water softens the soil.

Meadows are the most enduring and readily noticed landmarks, so identification of road forks and the relative situation of camps and other spots evolves around them. "Let's start our hike from the north corner of White Deer Meadow," "Our camp's on the east side of Preacher's Meadow, about a half-mile past the creek," or "Follow this road until you've crossed two creeks and a small meadow. The next meadow on the right is where the trail to Finnegan's Lake starts."

Because of their function as guideposts, large unnamed meadows are rare in even the most isolated sections of the high country. Many small meadows, only an acre or two in area, have names and are identified on maps. Names of the meadows derive from many sources. Some reflect the animal life observed by the first explorers who traversed the Sierra: Elk Meadow, Big Wolf Meadow, Bear Meadow, Cougar Meadow. Others carry the names of domestic animals that may once have been pastured in them regularly, or that figured in some incident shared by early travellers: Bull Meadow, Jackass Meadow, Dead Mule Meadow.

Still others were named for prospectors who camped or

built cabins on them, for timber crew bosses, for settlers who used them for grazing or who operated stagecoach stations beside them: Mears, Hawley, Smith, Jones, Franklin. There are meadows commemorating national holidays: Fourth of July Meadow, Thanksgiving Meadow, Easter Meadow; or notable public figures of a bygone era: Belden Meadow, Yankee Jim Meadow, Sutro Meadow, Wishon Meadow. Ethnic origins of men who once camped or mined or cut timber or built railroads in the area gave some meadows their names: China, French, Spanish, Dutch.

Meadow names come from prominent natural features: Sand Ridge, Black Rocks, Split Butte, Elephant's Head, White Rock. Characteristic vegetation gives a clue to the names of meadows such as Whitethorn, Buckbush, Azalea, Onion, Aspen. Names are derived from locally memorable happenings: Starvation Meadow, No Gold Meadow, Marriage Meadow, Runaway Meadow, Dead Man's Meadow. Named creeks and streams have taken their names from meadows or have loaned their names to them. Few mountain meadows are anonymous.

Virtually all the high-country meadows had their origin in one of two natural forces: glaciers or fires. During the glacial age, massive sheets of ice crept slowly, inexorably, over the up-thrusting close-grained granite bedrock that lies beneath most of the Sierra. In places, the unbelievable weight of the ice sheets gouged lake beds out of the rock; elsewhere the ice simply levelled the granite's corrugations. Where creeks flowed or springs rose, the depressions became lakes. Ultimately many of the lakes died from evaporation, but not until they had caught and held the debris that still sifts into high-country lakes: seeds and twigs from the valleys to the west, dust and sand from the arid lands to the east.

In some meadows where snowponds form each year, the process by which meadows were created during the passing of millenia can be seen compressed into a relatively short span of years. In these meadows the snowponds shrink steadily in size, and when a pond evaporates as summer wanes an examination of the soil at its edges reveals that there has been deposited around it a small ridge of waterborne and windborne debris, from a half foot to less than an inch high. In a decade, a pond that was once forty or fifty feet across may have shrunk in size by a third, as the level of the meadow at its rim is built up. Eventually, in a half-century or a century, the meadow will be uniformly level, and no pond will form at its edge or center.

Fire-created meadows almost always support some stands of bushes as well as grass, and these meadows generally are dotted with a few trees that somehow survived the blaze that destroyed the pine forest which once stood where the land is now open. The origin of a meadow can usually be told at first glance. Those in glacial saucers follow the contours of the bedrock that underlies their thin coating of soil, and slope gently from rim to center. Almost all glacial meadows are longer in one dimension than others and in almost all of them the long dimension is in line with the southward march of the slowly edging glacial ice.

Fire-created meadows tend to be flat, may even rise to a low center hump, and are often on a steep slope, a valley side or the slant of a ridge. The soil in glacial meadows is generally finer in texture than that in meadows created by an ancient burn, and in the latter the soil will be more thickly studded with big rocks.

Newcomers to the Sierra high country habitually fall in love with the whispering scented pine forests and ignore the meadows or overlook them. Most individuals just beginning to get acquainted with the Sierra associate towering groves of pines with towering peaks, and at the first cursory glance a meadow is a featureless flat, devoid of interest or activity. However, neither pine forest nor meadow can be ignored if the full flavor of the mountains is to be savored; one without the other is like an egg without a yolk, incomplete.

Lacking the flat surfaces of the meadows, where snow may pile up to a depth of thirty or forty feet during the long winter, and without the sponge of soil into which the snow-melt water seeps, the pine forest would wither and vanish. Meadows are the great conservators of water in the high country, where springs and creeks and rivers run for the most part along rocky channels to carry off much of the snow melt and rain water. Conversely, without the protection of the pines that surround them, the mountain meadows would be swept clear of earth by the dry winds of late summer, and would disappear. Without the birds and small animals that divide their time between meadows and forests, carrying seeds to caches and distributing them in their droppings, neither meadows nor pine groves would flourish and be renewed.

This is an oversimplification, of course. It stresses too strongly only a few of many interrelated forces that keep the Sierra Nevada range viable. None of these forces is cataclysmic, as was the folding and tilting and upheaving of the earth's crust that eons ago gave the mountains birth. Their life is maintained by more gentle forces working in subtler patterns, small and slow-working, delicately balanced, and precise forces that work imperceptibly, almost invisibly. Among these are the action of water and cold on stone; the falling of rain and snow; the cycle of seeds sprouting into plants that live for only a few weeks, even a few days; the movements and actions of birds and animals; the photosynthesis of the sunshine; the interreactions of acids and alkalies in the soil. The more obvious, more powerful forces are still at work as well: the lightning, the rain, the snow, the winds. These come from the ocean west of the range and the desert east of it.

Let us go back to the beginning. First there was a flat land, thinly covered with a layer of soil, through which sluggish streams meandered. Far beneath the soil's surface unimaginably great tensions formed in the earth's crust and when the tension became unbearable the crust fractured and buckled and relieved itself by thrusting upward. From unplumbed inner depths of the globe fissures carried to the surface white-hot magma that spurted in explosive orgasms over parts of the great, high, jagged scar the upheavals had created.

Time passed. The planet tilted on its axis, massive sheets of glacial ice came creeping over the sterile scar, smoothed its sharpest edges, broke into stones and pebbles the solid granite that had heaved from the depths and ground these

Except for sheltered drifts in groves where pine and fir branches interlace almost inextricably, the snow goes completely within a few days. The creeks seek the lakes and rivers that lie below the peaks.

into sand. The crawling ice scraped and shaped the granite, levelling here, smoothing there, splitting elsewhere, gouging pockets and ledges, giving form and feature to the hitherto shapeless rock. But after the glaciers had passed or melted, the rock remained barren, essentially sterile.

Rain came, and snow. Their water seeped into microscopic cracks in the granite, freezing and expanding in the cold air, opening fissures in which water courses formed. Over more centuries the erosion of running water created a coarse-textured soil lacking nutrients that would support life. Winds blew over the peaks from valley and desert, bringing dust that sifted down and intermingled with the coarse granitic sands. Birds flew over and left droppings that contained undigested seeds; the droppings contained minute quantities of nitrogen extracted from the birds' bodies, supplying the element of nutrition the thin soil lacked.

Supplied with nutrition, some of the seeds rooted and survived to grow into plants that flourished under the intense summer sun after the snow melted, and died when the snow returned. Under its white covering the cold worked on the dead plants, freezing and expanding their cells, breaking up their fibers. When the quick hot sun of summer came again the plants rotted swiftly and their shattered cells sank into the soil, carrying nitrates and phosphates, converting the sterile dirt into fertile life-supporting humus. On this enriched covering the seeds shed by plants and still deposited by birds found life and flourished, and in time's slow cycle the barren rocks came to be covered with green growth.

Small rodents came from the warm valleys on one side and from the dry mesas on the other, looking for food and for a protective covering under which they could live and breed. Mobile and active, these burrowers brought tree seeds from the valleys, alder and pine and cedar and hemlock, to cache in subterranean storehouses against the foodless winter. Not all the seeds were eaten. In caches only partly emptied or forgotten, some of them sprouted. Trees appeared, their roots fed by water trickling through the rodent burrows. During more millenia the trees cross-pollinated and mutated and evolved into new species adapted to the high altitudes at which they grew. Insects arrived, bark beetles and borers, to attack the weaker trees, and these died and fell, giving the healthy trees room in which to flourish; the boles and branches of the dead trees decayed and enriched and deepened the soil still more.

Birds followed the insects on which they fed. The small rodents attracted the furred predators that ate them. Deer and elk came up from the crowded valleys and plains, seeking new grazing grounds; they found them in the meadows, and found shelter in the forests that now covered the steep slopes. Large feral beasts trailed after the antlered breeds on which they preyed; bear and timber wolf, coyote and cougar, came to inhabit the high land.

Beaver arrived and built their dams across the narrow fast-coursing streams that had carried most of the snow-melt water away from the heights. From the ponds behind the dams the water sank into voids deep in the granite bedrock. These voids stored the water until they could hold no more; then their overflow trickled along underground fissures and faults and surfaced as bubbling springs. The springs created creeks and brooks that ran into depressions in the meadows and in the bare granite, and lakes appeared. With agonizing slowness, over an immeasurable period of time, the photosynthesis of sunshine mutated seeds and produced new kinds of plant life, and inbreeding created new species of animals and birds. Still other life forms migrated up the slopes from the warm rich overcrowded valleys and from the arid desert. The mountains came to life.

Nature did not allow them to come into life without struggling. Diseases decimated the animals, carrying off the weakest; the less-sturdy plants attracted blights that thinned the vegetation both in forests and meadows. Lightning flashed and started fires that bared great areas of the mountainsides. Manzanita rooted on the burned slopes and fed upon itself, its leaves and branches falling around its roots to nourish them in the flame-seared soil. Into the thorny manzanita thickets rodents and birds carried tree seeds. Saplings sprouted and grew big, overshadowed the manzanita and caused it to die. The forest regenerated itself.

In the craters of dead volcanoes and in the glacial saucers where they had formed, lakes filled with windblown debris and disappeared. Where the lakes had been, meadows spread. Running water moved soil and seeds to places where neither had been before. In the soil the seeds sprouted and vegetation spread. At the bases of cliffs the moving water merged into streams that carved the valleys deeper. The sides and floors of the valleys became green and fertile.

When men first came to the Sierra Nevada, the range was already formed, bulking immense and seemingly immune to human ravaging. The first men to pass were few in number and had for tools only primitive axes with heads chipped from stone, and branches with tips sharpened and hardened by fire with which to break the soil. These aboriginals found the mountains too inhospitable an environment; they stayed a very short time and left few traces of their presence. However, in only a few years as mountain life is measured, humans have in quick surges increased their ability to multiply the power of their puny muscles. They come now with machines that tear into the Sierra's flanks.

Unaided, human strength cannot damage the mountains, but the devices that combine the labor of many men working in foundries and factories multiply the strength of a few into a force that can do damage. Without their machines, without the chemicals created in their laboratories, men cannot destroy or even greatly damage the fragile balances required to sustain the mountain wilderness. But when human muscles are multiplied many thousandfold, they have a power against which the slowly-working forces of nature are defenseless. The argument is often advanced that the mountains are there for humans to use, and in order for them to be used, they must be tamed. Taming for use is one thing; in the immediate past, the words "use" and "taming" have too often become euphemisms for "destruction." Even at this writing, machines and chemicals are altering the natural balances arrived at by uncounted centuries of trial and error and maintained by nature in precarious balance.

Somewhere there lies a sensible compromise between nature's vulnerable resources and men's access to the beauty of the mountains, a compromise that will not upset natural adjustments made in the course of ages. Those who scoff at the suggestion that the mountains are vulnerable and can be destroyed need only to look at the lands bordering the Mediterranean. In writings of those who saw them only a few centuries ago they are described as thickly forested, green, pulsing with animal life; now, they are rocky, treeless, semiarid deserts. Surely there is a middle ground between those who would use the mountains indiscriminately and those who would banish all human activity from the wilds. The use of natural resources by what we call civilization cannot be summarily halted, but neither ought it be continued without controls.

Even such a simple man-created work as a road can be an agency that upsets natural balances in the high country. There are many roads and trails here, some still travelled after two hundred years. As long as these were used only by travellers on foot or by animal-powered vehicles, they did little harm to the areas they penetrated. Now, the old roads give access to vehicles with powerful motors that tear away the soil and change natural watershed patterns by creating ruts in which new run-offs form. Some of these new patterns bring death to creeks that run in centuries-old beds. When the machines leave the roads they can break the thin soil-crust and allow it to be swept away by wind and water, destroying vegetation, driving out animals and birds by razing the coverts in which they shelter and depriving them of the food they need for survival. The damage may already be irreversible, beyond the subtle forces of nature to repair.

Suggestions are often made that those genuinely interested in enjoying the beauty and serenity of wild unspoiled places should not be afraid to enter such places on nature's own terms, using their own muscles unaided by machines. The makers as well as the possessors of these machines scoff at such suggestions and battle efforts to place restrictions on their use. They argue that people, too, are part of nature—carefully avoiding mention of machines—and hold that somehow nature will repair the damage the machines cause. Sadly, the proponents of both arguments are intransigent, and seem more interested in maintaining their fixed positions than in finding areas of agreement.

This much can be said: we as a nation must find a solution to this national problem. The Sierra is not the only endangered area; what is true of this range is true of other places. Unregulated activities in the Sierra range, in the foothills, the high country, and the High Sierra, can irreparably upset the precise natural balance that brought the range into being and maintains its life.

The Sierra can be destroyed. In spite of an accelerated program of study and research into ecological problems, our knowledge of natural cause and effect is still far from total. We should be everything except arrogant and over-positive in our assumption that our acquired knowledge is superior to long natural processes.

The lake is small, so small that at first we thought it to be an oversized snow pond.

Examples speak louder than flat statements. When we first began our explorations of the Sierra high country in the 1930s, extensive areas of the pine forest were being attacked by blister rust, a disease that arrived in a shipment of pine seedlings from Europe in the early 1900s. By 1920 the infection had spread widely, and before its control was begun nearly twenty years later, most of the Sierra western white pines were dead or dying. The long delay was not due to inertia; efforts to control the blight could not begin until researchers discovered methods by which it could be arrested.

All that was known of the disease when it first appeared was that airborne spores carried it into the trees. The spores settled on the bark, penetrated it and killed it in great patches, cutting off the flow of sap. Remember the care the sapsucker takes never to girdle a tree with its bill? The trees struck by blister rust were girdled as effectively as if the job had been done with axe or saw. Young trees just past the seedling stage were the most vulnerable, and great stands of such trees, potential forests, were completely wiped out before the cycle of infection was uncovered. The only results produced by early research were negative: no chemical then known had any effect on the spores.

When researchers began studying the spores in forests instead of laboratories, they found that for a year the blister rust spores lie dormant in a host plant, the gooseberry bush or currant bush, instead of propagating on trees or spreading from tree to tree. Once this was confirmed, the solution became a matter of logic: eliminate the host and the blister rust spores would disappear. Though logical, the method was time-consuming. The job of grubbing out millions of gooseberry and currant bushes from the forest floor began during the late 1930s, was interrupted by World War II, and was resumed shortly thereafter. While this work was in progress, it was impossible to visit any pine-forested Sierra area without seeing heavy white cords outlining the clumps of bushes that were to be eradicated, or encountering the crews that were doing the grubbing-out.

For almost fifteen years the laborious task of uprooting by hand all of the bushes that hosted the blister rust spore went on. The project was finally closed out and labelled "finished," and blister rust has now vanished from among the pines. Isolated gooseberry and currant bushes are beginning to sprout once more, though. If the rust reappears, the job may need to be done a second time.

Now, this brings up a series of tricky "what if?" questions. What if, in the beginning days of the eradication program, the defoliants and herbicides now being used had been available? Because the grubbing was selective, it had to be done by hand, muscle power aided only by a grubbing hoe. What if small machines that are available today could have been used instead of the simple hand tools that were used?

Consider the possibilities. Only after years of using such relatively new compounds as atrizine, nitralin, diphenamid and similar herbicides, and such potent insecticides as DDT and malathion are their side effects being uncovered. Belatedly, we are learning the harm some chemical compounds do to soil fertility, to all forms of life. Suppose that a chemical, then untested for long-term effects, had been seized on as a miraculous answer to blister rust? Suppose further that the side effects of its use proved damaging, even fatal, to plant and animal life, and this discovery came too late? The suppositions are not far-fetched. Even in an age when computers and electron microscopes accelerate research, we belatedly discover that some widely-used chemicals have unforeseen long-term effects on all life, plant, animal, bird, fish, human. Three or four decades ago, widespread use of an unknown compound might have exposed all life in the Sierra to a slowly-acting poison that would have denuded the mountains.

Enough problems already face the fragile Sierran ecology. We cannot afford to waste time exploring theoretical answers to rhetorical questions; too many such questions reflect fantasy, not reality. The immediate problem is to insure that the natural balances of the range are not damaged by unwise use of its resources. Harvesting the Sierra's trees and ores and providing access to campers, hikers, hunters and anglers can be brought into harmony with the ecological needs of the mountains. After this problem has been solved, answers can be sought to the more complex questions of long-term use and preservation.

Older problems were much simpler. They concerned such things as fire control, which still remains a problem. No ingenious machine has yet been devised that will replace the muscles of men working with simple hand tools in direct confrontation with the fierce heat of a forest fire.

Forest fires are dreadful things, and those caused by the careless, the lazy or ignorant, and most recently the arsonist somehow seem more dreadful than those set by a natural force such as lightning. They are not, of course. All forest fires are equally tragic, but they are a part of the system of balanced forces created by nature long before men came to the mountains. Then, fires burned themselves out, and over slow decades the burned-over areas underwent the regenerative cycles of reclamation. Manzanita brush came first, growing swiftly to cover and anchor the loose soil. Seeds dropped by birds and animals restored the pines among the manzanita brush. The trees grew tall and shaded the brush, which died because it will not survive shaded places. Left to itself, nature will restore the land; our trouble is impatience. We think nature's methods too slow.

Exposure to a forest fire is a dreadful experience nobody forgets: the shroud of acrid smoke that surrounds a fire area; the beating heat while still far distant from the heart of the blaze; the heavy, ominous terror-laden air that extends for many miles around.

Anyone who has walked through a newly burned area, feet uncushioned by the familiar springiness of soft forest-floor duff, surrounded by the skeletons of trees that rise like charred accusing fingers, must shudder at the thought of fire in the forest and admire the courage of the men who go into the burning area to control and extinguish it.

But fires burn openly and visibly, and can be fought in the open. They are less to be feared than other disruptive forces, too many of which are unleashed by humans with machines and chemicals. These subtle disruptions work unseen, their dangers unrecognized until the damage has become irreversible. We need to fear them more than we fear fires.

S THE MALL ANIMALS

EIGHT

S mall-animal life in the high country around the lake is highly visible, but more than a quick glance is required to see the most important parts of the lives of the small furred creatures which live on the meadows and among the trees. The occasional or unobservant visitor sees chipmunks and ground squirrels in profusion, less often a chickaree or marmot, and frequently fails to realize that what is seen is a very small portion of the whole panorama. Most of the small animals do not advertise their presence by venturing out during daylight hours, and there are a few who do not emerge even at night.

Mice and woodrats are the most numerous of the nocturnals. On the meadows where ground squirrels feed by day, the meadow mice take over at night. In the clearings chipmunks and ground squirrels feed from dawn to dusk, darting in antic scamperings. In the pine forests where chipmunks are joined by chickarees and a few squirrels, the deer mice and woodrats make their secret nests and come out of them only after darkness has fallen. Between the meadows and trees, moles and pocket gophers dig their tunnels, and while signs of their work are often present, the animals themselves are seldom seen.

Of the small animals that prey on their vegetarian cousins, only the weasel and badger hunt both by day and night. Others, marten, red mink, the rare red mountain fox, fisher and ringtail, do their hunting exclusively at night, when the mice and woodrats that are their favorite foods also go abroad. The larger predators, bobcats and coyotes and cougars, are also nighttime hunters, but theirs is another story.

So is that of the marmot. Marmots in isolated areas such as that surrounding the lake are not as shy as those which make their dens close to habited places. Marmots in settled and well-travelled places are often seen beside trails and roads, but disappear as if by magic when a person appears. Those that have little contact with humans are not as shy, and those that den close to the lake are surprisingly tolerant. They sit on the rocks a short distance from camp, taking the sunshine, and are either unmindful of our movements or undisturbed by them. Those living along the edge of the meadow in storm-windrowed broken tree boles let us walk up to within a dozen feet of them.

As long as we take short, shuffling steps and make no unnecessary noises, the marmot will sit calmly, cocking its head from side to side and tilting it back now and then to peer nearsightedly along its curved nose. If we stop before we get too close and stand quietly without talking or raising an arm or hand, the marmot will inspect us with the same curiosity we show in inspecting him. This silent mutual scrutiny may last a quarter of an hour before one of us makes the small involuntary movement that sends the marmot diving into its den.

Marmots are often called woodchucks or groundhogs, justifiably, as they belong to the same family. The yellow-bellied marmot of the Sierra high country is not identical with the eastern woodchuck, though. Locally and colloquially, marmots go by the name of "whistle-pigs," from their shrill call, which resembles the sound a gap-toothed youth makes when whistling through his front teeth. Marmots are hibernators, moving late in summer to a hidden den under a rocky outcrop or forest windfall, returning early to the meadows.

Soon after the snow melt begins and the babies that have been born during hibernation are big enough to get around, marmots take up their surface lives. The small marmots grow rapidly. During the first few weeks of the summer they can be seen, supervised by a parent, playing and feeding on the snow-patched meadows, always near the entrance of their summer burrow. Soon after midsummer it becomes difficult to distinguish young marmot from parent, and before winter arrives the young have cut family ties and gone to establish their own dens with their own mates. Marmots are gentle, harmless creatures, and since there are no gardens in the high country for them to invade they have not yet become objects for rifle target practice. Perhaps they never will.

Unusually keen eyes are not needed to find traces of deer mice and brush mice, in spite of their knack for staying invisible. The brush mouse is the shier of the two; it shuns both daylight and human-inhabited spots, but its droppings and the seed pods it has emptied and discarded during its nocturnal forays are widely scattered at the edges of most brushfields.

Deer mice, or white-footed mice, are also nocturnal, but their omnivorous appetites and their insatiable curiosity send them hunting in camps and cabins within a distance of several hundred yards from their woodpecker-hole homes. Their visits are made during the night's early hours, soon after campers have gone to bed. If the camp is a slovenly one, being used by those who have not taken the precaution of disposing of all table-scraps and putting all edibles into glass or metal containers, the noises made by the mice will usually rouse a sleeping human. No animal of any size is quite as noisy as a two-inch-long deer mouse tearing open a paper bag or cardboard carton or foil-wrapped parcel to get at whatever food these might hold.

Even when bathed in the glare of a flashlight snapped on by a camper awakened by the mouse's rustlings, deer mice seldom run. They stop tearing at the package that has drawn their interest, settle back on their strange stubby tails and sit blinking for a few seconds, then go back to ripping into the package that has attracted them. The sound of bedclothes being rustled, even the metallic hiss of a sleeping bag being zipped open, will seldom cause a deer mouse to run. If the awakened camper finally drags himself out of bed, the mouse will wait until its involuntary host is a foot or less away before disappearing.

Human voices alarm them, though. We once threw things at invading deer mice, but soon learned that it was only necessary to scold them. A few quiet words in a conversational tone, or even a whisper, sends them into immediate retreat. Once alarmed, the mice will seldom return during the same night, but if food is not properly stored or if the least table scraps are not burned or buried, the mice will be back the next night and the next night and the next, as long as there's a scrap to be gathered. Deer mice will eat anything. Testing their appetites, we've left such unlikely delicacies as onions, red peppers, chocolate, ham, peppermints and similar unmouselike foods carefully wrapped in various coverings; only soap was refused.

Deer mice and brush mice belong to the same family, but can be told apart very easily, for the deer mouse has a tail shorter than its body, one of the few species that do. In coloring, the two are quite similar; their body fur shades from a light brown along their backs to golden tan on their flanks, both have white underbody fur, white legs and feet. The chances are good if you are camping in the high country and are awakened by a rustling of paper or wrapping-foil that it is a deer mouse taking advantage of your careless hospitality.

Meadow mice belong to the harvest mouse family, and it is hard to get a good look at them. Evidence that the little nocturnals are active in a given meadow, though, can be found quite easily by daylight. Meadow mice make runways, narrow paths at the grass-roots level, much as they tunnel through snow during the winter months. These grass tunnels are barely one mouse wide, an inch or less, and are hidden from view from above by the tall grass stalks that lean together. To find the tunnels, part the grass gently until you discover one, then you can easily follow it. Be prepared for it to lead you to the meadow's edge and vanish, but orient yourself so that you can return to the same spot in the dark.

Flashlight in hand, go back to the meadow an hour or so after sundown. You will already have selected a spot where the tunnels in the grass are thickest and the grass is thinnest; the ideal spot will be almost bare. When you reach your lookout point, kneel down and remain quiet for about a quarter-hour. Time will pass more slowly than you think, so consult your watch—without using your flash, of course. Now, lower the flash to the ground, or an inch or so above it,

The dusky-footed wood rat builds his winter home of grass stems and small twigs, carefully interwoven into a beautifully symmetrical dome that, like the thatched roof of a cottage, will shed water.

aimed at the spot you've already chosen. Push the button, and with luck there will be a meadow mouse or two caught in the light's beam.

If there isn't, wait a while and try again. Sooner or later, you'll see one, though there's little about the meadow mouse that is radically different from any other dun-colored mouse, except that it's more elusive than most. Meadow mice have dusky grey-brown body fur and their underbodies are a soft pearl grey. If you do get the overwhelming urge to look at one, it will closely resemble the common house mouse of civilization.

Only one of the small mountain rodents makes a surface nest. The dusky-footed woodrat begins in late summer to construct its new home; last winter's was abandoned when the snow melted, and during the summer the woodrat has made its home in any convenient crevice it happened to be near when bedtime came, about an hour before sunrise. For winter, the woodrat builds a beautifully symmetrical dome of grass stems and small twigs carefully interwoven, laid down with painstaking care and accuracy so that the dome, like the thatched roof of a cottage, will shed water. At some point around the circular perimeter of its nest the rat leaves an opening about an inch above ground; this is its doorway. The floor is covered deeply enough with grass to assure that the mouse will stay dry if a temporary melt occurs after the first snow. When the snow is deep enough the rat will tunnel through it from his doorway and extend the tunnels to buried grass heads that provide its winter diet of seeds. By summer, the original tunnel will have grown into a maze.

Moles and pocket gophers are seen even more rarely than meadow mice and woodrats, for they emerge only oc-

With the beginning of summer and the melting of snow, the round-humped gently-curved rises on the ground are shown to be mole-runs.

casionally from their underground runs either by night or by day. Their lives are spent almost entirely below ground. They work daily, extending their tunnels, feeding on the roots of grasses and shrubs and wildflowers, and on the grubs and earthworms that are curled up in many of the root clumps.

Both moles and gophers emerge on occasion during the darkest hours of night to spend short periods outside their burrows, but they are exceedingly sensitive to vibrations transmitted through the earth, and a distant footfall will send them diving back underground. Vibrations appear to cause both moles and gophers to suspend digging; there is evidence that the big mountain cats as well as coyotes and badgers can hear or feel this digging, locate its source, and break into the tunnels from above.

Especially when summer is beginning and the snow melt taking place, the work of moles and gophers is very apparent. As the white ground cover diminishes the mole runs can be seen in round-humped, gently curved rises on the ground; when the snow lies deep the moles work only an inch or so underground and the gophers tunnel between snow and soil. Mole runs often collapse the moment the snow softens, and gopher tunnels show early during the melt; the warm air softens the snow above them and lays them bare before the rest of the ground has been uncovered.

Moles soften the earth at their tunnel faces with their short, heavily clawed forefeet and periodically dig at right angles to their main tunnel. The lateral is dug upward and the plug of dirt created by digging the main tunnel is pushed up and out onto the surface, where it forms a mound. Gophers also dig laterals, but turn inside their tunnels and scoop the loosened dirt of the main burrow out of the lateral to form an open conical dump. The different styles of the two burrows make it easy to distinguish between their work. The surface hole is plugged by moles, left open by gophers.

All the burrowing animals, moles, gophers, mice, woodrats, ground squirrels, and marmots, are the great irrigators of the high country's slopes. Through their tunnels the snow-melt water is distributed to the roots of thirsty trees and shrubs and grass, their deep runs carry the moisture far down, where it pools and does not evaporate under the bright sun. Without the conduits the burrowers provide, the invaluable water from the summer melt would rush uncontrolled into the beds of creeks, be fed to the rivers, and carried out to mingle with the salt water of the ocean. Without the water retained in the soil by the burrowers' activities, the high country would be brown and sere instead of fertile green.

Ground squirrels and chipmunks are the most visible of the Sierra's small mammals. The golden mantled ground squirrel, which looks more like a chipmunk than its monochromatically furred relative, the Belding, is as bold as the chipmunks in its readiness to fraternize with humans. The Belding ground squirrel is frequently mistaken for a gopher by those who have never seen gophers. The Belding is much more timid and retiring than the golden mantled, perhaps because it does not climb trees and lacks the security the golden mantled and chipmunks have in being able to escape in a flash by running up the nearest pine-bole.

Belding ground squirrels live in the meadows, golden mantleds at the edges of the trees; their burrows are often made inside of the root system of a blasted pine or below the overhang of a big deadfall. The Beldings forage incessantly on the meadows and in the clearings for the seeds and tender grass heads which are their main food. When people approach, or when the shadow of a hunting hawk passes over the meadow, the squirrels dive into the nearest burrow—their own or one made by another squirrel—amid a chorus of shrill squeaky whistlings. Their timidity is in unending contest with their curiosity. Quick to dive underground, they are equally quick to pop their heads back up for a look around.

Unless there is an obvious source of danger nearby, the ground squirrel will search its surroundings for a few moments with its head protruding from the burrow. Once satisfied that all is safe, it pops out and stands erect on the mounded earth around the hole for a few seconds before starting to feed again. It can hold this standing position almost indefinitely, its tiny body erect, forepaws folded over chest, looking for all the world like a snag root or the tip of a windfelled branch. Sierra pioneers were quick to see the resemblance between the Belding and a stake driven into the ground; thus in a period when horses were often staked out with picket pins, the Belding acquired its alias of "picket pin squirrel" among high-country dwellers.

An inquisitive person wanting to watch these little fellows needs only to walk a few yards out on a meadow where they are active and settle down in a comfortable position. After a few minutes, the ground squirrels that shot underground at the approach of a stranger will begin to pop their heads out of the mounded burrow-mouths. They will duck back, and reappear, but will not come out at once. If the squir-

The timid and retiring Belding ground squirrel forages incessantly on the meadows and in the clearings for the seeds and tender grass-heads which make up its main diet (right). The golden mantled ground squirrel stands erect, searching the surrounding area for any signs of danger (left).

rel-watcher sits still, however, they will climb up on their mounds and sit erect, matching his motionlessness, and after a cautionary interval will begin to eat and move around freely once again.

There may be some sort of pecking order, seniority of a fashion, among the Belding ground squirrels. Not all of them will leave their burrows at once. Two or three will begin to move, but only inches from the safety of their tunnels. They usually dust-bathe first, spreadeagling their bellies on the ground around the burrow entry, rubbing themselves into the loose soil so diligently that they form small depressions in which they roll and squirm. After bathing they stand erect and massage their bodies with their forepaws and shake themselves to get rid of the dust in their fur. If the watcher still holds his position, the Beldings soon resume feeding, and once the leaders have started to eat, the remainder of the colony emerge a few at a time until the meadow is a busy scene again.

Hunting hawks understand this ground squirrel habit. A hawk that has cruised at low altitude of fifteen or twenty feet over a meadow and seen its shadow send the Beldings to cover will perch low in the trees at its edge, or perhaps in a clump of willows if there is a stream that cuts through the meadow. The bird takes a position in the foliage to blur its shadow and keep its silhouette from being noticeable against the sky. The perch will be as low as possible, just far enough from the ground to let the hawk gain the speed it needs to swoop quickly. There the bird waits until the squirrels have forgotten its threat, until they have made their preliminary reconnoitre and started to feed. Then the hawk swoops down and takes the squirrel closest to its perch.

A human observer need only match the hawk's patience to see the meadow soon resume its normal rhythm. Scores of the ground squirrels begin to dot its expanse. Some are hidden in the taller grass clumps, the only sign of their activity being the twitching of the seed-heavy grass stems. Others feed at the edges of bare spots. They move from clump to clump, selecting a grass stem with as much care as a French chef uses in choosing fresh vegetables from a market stall.

Having found a stalk with a rich cluster of seeds at its tip, the squirrel brings itself erect, often rearing up to the very tips of its hind paws, and pulls the stem down with a paw-over-paw movement resembling that of a man hauling on a rope. When the tip is within reach, the ground squirrel settles back on its haunches, body erect, and nibbles seeds until the stalk is denuded, before moving along to look for another.

Unlike the retiring Belding ground squirrel, the golden mantled species is as gregarious as the chipmunks it so closely resembles. The heads of golden mantleds are covered with fur of a rich orange shade, which extends down below their shoulders. Like chipmunks, their body fur is deep tan and their backs marked with alternate stripes of black and white. Like chipmunks in another way, the golden mantled ground squirrels prefer to live at the edges of small rock-strewn clearings among the pines. They do not climb trees in chipmunk-style, but are as earthbound as their Belding cousins and confine their scamperings to the trunks of windfalls.

Around the lake we see three of the half-dozen Sierra chipmunk species. The tiny lodgepole chipmunk predominates, sharing territory with the larger Allen and the relatively scarce long-eared chipmunk. All the chipmunks are marked quite similarly, with back stripes and body dots of fur darker than the deep fawn shade which covers their backs and flanks. They can be distinguished most easily by size and head formation.

All chipmunks are fearless of man and quickly accept human presence in their territory. They are secure to the point of arrogance in the knowledge that their agility will enable them to elude not only humans but generally the animal hunters as well. Only one of its feral enemies, the weasel, can chase a chipmunk with any success. The other small tree-climbing predators, mink and marten, chase chipmunks if they see a likely target when they come out at dusk to hunt, but most of the chipmunks retire early. A majority of those caught by marten or mink are taken in their nests at night.

Chipmunks leap for the closest tree when alarmed or chased. They have a foot formation that makes them almost uncatchable; on both forepaws and hindpaws, one back claw is set at right angles to the others and the chipmunk can swivel this claw to descend a tree headfirst. Squirrels, chickarees and weasels have similar foot formations. All three can move as well as chipmunks in the trees, climbing up or scrambling laterally around a tree trunk, or descending headfirst. Mink and marten climb readily, but when descending

All the chipmunks are marked quite similarly, with back stripes and body dots of dark fur.

must go around the trunk in a spiral, their bodies horizontal. A chipmunk dashes down headfirst at full speed.

Even weasels are hard-put to catch a chipmunk that is alerted to its presence before the weasel springs. Most of the chipmunks that weasels chase into trees escape by picking their paths over twigs too flimsy to carry the weasel's weight. If the weasel gets too close and the chipmunk makes the mistake of trying to find safety in a deserted woodpecker hole, its life is forfeit. The weasel's long sinuous body is very little bigger in diameter than a chipmunk's; it can enter even the small tunnels of rats and mice. If a marten or mink chases a chipmunk into a woodpecker hole, the hunter will wait with the implacable patience of all feral animals, clinging to the bark or poised on a tree branch beside the hole, until the chipmunk extends its head to see if the coast is clear. Unless a larger animal has spooked the mink or marten, the coast seldom is.

"Cute" is a word often used to describe chipmunks, and indeed they are. They are bold in their approach to humans and in allowing people to get close to them. When we first set up camp, the chipmunks and golden mantleds keep their distance for a few days, suitably cautious of our presence, until they discover that we mean them no harm. After that, our movements disturb them only when we happen onto one which hasn't noticed our approach, in which case the startled animal dashes away. But generally we go about our business and the chipmunks attend to theirs.

Chipmunks are avid eaters and great food-storers, and this together with their fearlessness makes them easy to tame. We do not really approve of feeding them regularly, for fear they will get accustomed to depending on us for their needs and become the forest equivalent of welfare cases. But we do feed them, and though we do not work consciously at taming them, those with nests close by soon become quite friendly. They scamper up to us to receive a breadcrumb or a chip of cracker, eat the tidbit and wash, scouring their small pointed faces with forepaws that they have moistened with a flickering tongue. Occasionally we have a few peanuts to offer them, and these they prefer to store, after eating one or two as a sample. When offered more, they pack the nuts into their cheek pouches and scurry off to add them to one of their many caches.

Few animals are drones, living off the land but contributing nothing in return; chipmunks are noteworthy for returning far more to the Sierra than they take as food. Each year they plant more trees than does the U. S. Forest Service and all the private timber companies combined, and as an added bonus they also plant grass and flower seeds. The cheek pouches of a chipmunk are astonishingly capacious; they hold hundreds of grass or flower seeds and as many as twenty-five or thirty big seeds from pinecones. The chipmunk buries the seeds in shallow holes for its winter food supply, small caches only an inch or two in diameter and an inch or less below the surface. Each year, a chipmunk forgets the location of about a third of its caches; the seeds in these take root and spread both trees and meadow plants into areas they might not otherwise reach.

Chickarees, the other highly visible small Sierra animals, are generally mistaken for squirrels and usually called squirrels, but actually belong to a separate species. There are some grey squirrels in the high country, but few of them are anything except summer visitors. Some winter above the snow line, but generally squirrels will stay at 6,000 feet or below. Chickarees reverse this; they rarely go below 6,000 feet and their range extends on up to the 10,000-foot level.

In appearance, chickarees strongly resemble squirrels but are smaller and have a different head configuration. Squirrels have conical heads with pointed muzzles; chickarees' jaws are triangular in relation to the tops of their heads and their muzzles are flat. The bushy tail of a squirrel is the same color as its body fur, while a chickaree has a dark brush, grey to black, tipped with the same white that these little creatures have on their underbodies.

Chickarees are both quarrelsome and curious. When any animal or human enters its forest territory, a chickaree begins an angry chattering and keeps up this flow of invective until the intruder is identified as friend or enemy. Humans can pass the test for friendliness by sitting down or leaning against a tree and remaining quite still while the chickaree comes to investigate. It usually scampers up to within a few feet of the intruder, perches on a log or stump or low branch, and inspects the stranger for several minutes before going about its business with a flick of its bushy tail and a treble-toned *chirk*. Although chickarees keep up an almost constant chattering as they move around, they are quiet when eating or resting. If the forest is silent, a few short whistles will usually bring any chickaree in the vicinity to investigate the source of the strange sound.

Like chipmunks, chickarees cache food for winter. From the time the pinecones begin to mature in midsummer until long after the first snowfall, chickarees cut the cones, dropping several from each tree before descending. Then, perched on a log or stump, they pick up the cones and gnaw the scales away from their fibrous cores, much as a person would eat corn off the cob. After the cone has been cleared the chickaree strips away the leathery outer husk from the scales and extracts the sweet inner seed. Cone cores and scale husks dropped as they eat form untidy little "chickaree middens." The middens and the sound of their whistled calls are the best clues to the presence of chickarees in a pine grove. Seeds not eaten at once are stored by the animal near its nest tree. Like chipmunks, chickarees forget the location of many of their caches each year, and seeds left in them sprout into seedlings.

Since chickarees do not hibernate as do most small mammals that winter in the high country, a cozy nest is essential to their survival during the long season of snow and cold. Nest building reaches its peak during the early days of summer, in preparation for the birth of new litters in July, but the chickarees always seem to be at work, either building new nests in abandoned woodpecker holes or improving old ones. Much of the late-summer nest building is done by young chickarees. Launched on their own five to six weeks after they are born, the young instinctively prepare for winter. But even in late summer adult chickarees are seen hurrying around with a bunch of soft moss or grass in their mouths, improving the bedding in an existing nest.

Chickarees are both quarrelsome and curious, keeping up an angry chattering until an intruder has been identified as friend or foe.

It's hard to avoid the pitfall of anthropomorphism when watching the day-active small animals of the high country. Though less obvious than simians in their resemblance to humans, at some point in their activities the ground squirrels, chipmunks and chickarees all display traits that we consider humanoid. A Belding ground squirrel wrestling down a stalk of grass both looks and moves like a man standing on tiptoe while hauling on a rope; a chipmunk hunkered down washing its face passes its forepaws over its cheeks and muzzle in the fashion of someone splashing water on his face from a basin; a chickaree gnawing seed scales from a pinecone eats in the style of a person enjoying corn on the cob. When watching these and some of the other actions of the little animals it's often necessary to remind oneself that they are being guided by instinct, not reason. Shortly thereafter, the sobering thought occurs that this is also true of many human actions.

THE
TOWNS & PEOPLE
NINE

S taying for an extended time in an isolated area of the Sierra is a sovereign cure for wastefulness. Soon after we set up camp, while getting reacquainted with the pine forest on one side of the lake and the meadow and ridges on the other, we note the location of the nearest dry windfalls that are suitable for cutting into firewood. There is no lack of windfelled trees in early summer, but not all of them are at the right stage of drying. For its wood to burn best, a windfelled pine must lie on the ground three to four years. Until it has air-dried for three years, pine is too full of sap; it makes a slow, spitting, smoky fire. After it has dried five years or more, the wood burns too hot and too fast.

In early years, we learned to judge how long a windfall had been on the ground by the condition of its bark and the feel of the saw cutting through it. As years passed, we came to know the location of the grounded trees and could remember about when they had toppled. We have never been forced to cut a tree during all the years we have camped at the lake, but we often chop down a sapling that is one of a spindly lot trying to survive in the shade of a grove. Only a small percentage of these struggling young trees grow to maturity; they do not flourish unless they are bathed in sunlight, something that happens to relatively few trees in a big, dense stand.

At the beginning of our stay we are prodigal of wood, but as the weeks go by and it becomes necessary to search further and further away from camp for suitable deadfalls, our consumption slows down. This experience is shared by all campers who stay in one spot for a long while. There is always the thought of the work involved in restocking the woodpile. Each limb must be dragged back, so before cutting a limb off its bole with the bowsaw, we give it careful study. A branch that is very crooked and gnarled is hard to drag, even over level ground that is sparsely bushed. If a limb has lost most of its twigs, then kindling must come from other sources, which means additional searching. Finally, the limb must not be too big, or it will be beyond the strength of one man to handle.

Our fires gradually become more and more frugal. The blaze is fed with greater precision, using no more sticks than are necessary to yield a satisfactory bed of coals. Each stick added to the fire is handled with the memory of the labor it represents, sawing the limb off its bole, dragging it to camp, sawing or reducing it to length with the axe, splitting big butt-chunks into several small sticks so they will catch faster and burn more evenly. Chunks too big for a beginning blaze and yet too small to split are set aside for use after the meal has been cooked; one or two of them are added to the bed of coals to burn until bedtime, and their size and number is carefully gauged so that they will be consumed by then. No bit of wood is wasted.

Frugality is also our watchword in cooking as the days pass. We do not have parsimonious meals or stint ourselves, but we know the larder is limited and will diminish steadily, while our appetites stay constant. We create tasty dishes from leftovers and odds and ends, using every scrap of food, delaying the time when a trip must be made to one of the nearest mountain towns to replenish the grub-box. By the time our supplies are almost totally depleted, we have become so accustomed to the high country's peaceful days and nights that we have begun to feel strangely detached from civilization. We have no great desire to visit settled places, even though the two mountain towns nearest the lake are free from the clamor and oppressive crowding of cities.

Each of the two towns offers about the same choice of stores and supplies at about the same average prices. Each has the same facilities: a filling station–general store, a short-order restaurant, a bar. They are about equal in size, both under five hundred population, and equally distant from our camp. Our choice is much the same whether we turn right or left when we reach the paved highway. The two towns even have similar histories. Both were settled in the mid-1850s, when the tide of gold seekers had washed up the foothills from the west and over the Sierra's crest. In their earliest days both of the towns were populated by miners; the miners were replaced by timber workers when gold gave way to logging, and both have now shrunk greatly. During the timber era both towns boomed, and well-built homes replaced the shacks that had formed them in their beginnings. Then the boom died, men were replaced by machines on the logging stands, and the towns dwindled rapidly.

There are a dozen towns much like these two that cling to the Sierra's eastern flank, and all of them share the same ambivalence. Most of them have a highway in common, the single well-paved road that curves along the mountainsides, two lanes wide, three on a very few steep grades where the big trucks must crawl with down-shifted gears. The road is classed as a secondary highway, a relatively unimportant link between the transcontinental interstate thoroughfares that run east and west. Though it is the only road linking the interstates for fifty to sixty miles in either direction, it parallels other secondary links that have fewer weather problems during the winter months.

Despite its secondary status, the highway is the chief artery leading to the unpaved roads that give access to the unsettled high country. Because of its secondary rating, it is among the last roads to be reopened after a major storm. The snowplows that give instant attention to the trans-Sierra freeways and the secondary roads that lead to ski resorts are not diverted from these high-priority missions to clear the secondary road which serves only a few small communities.

During any given winter, the eastern slope's highway is likely to be blocked by drifts on three or four occasions and closed for between three days and a week each time. The towns along it are isolated from both the outside areas and from one another, and this isolation includes in most cases the loss of such facilities as electric power and telephones. While the inhabitants of these high-country towns are not given to complaining, it would be impossible for them not to feel that they, like the road, are relegated to secondary status. The result is that most of them have developed a high degree of self-reliance and a thinly concealed contempt for those who elect to live in more populous and better-served places.

Casual visitors often make the mistake of writing off the citizens of the mountain towns as self-centered, ignorant, resentful bumpkins. They are not. They are keenly aware of world events, and from their isolation often view them with more objectivity and commonsense than do residents of metropolitan centers.

It is because they are objective that the residents of high-country towns both fear and resent what in large cities is considered progress. They foresee the time when a freeway will gash along the route their narrow secondary road now follows, and know this means that the present trickle of summer visitors will become a flood, with all the backwash of silt and debris that any flood brings.

This fear is reflected in their attitude toward the relatively few visitors who find their way to these communities during the short summer. Tourists are welcomed with a hospitality that soon freezes if the residents recognize them as types they consider undesirable. These types include the braggart psuedo-sportsman, the tin-can camper, the seeker of the superficially picturesque, and the metropolitan dweller who patronizingly find the high-country hamlets "quaint," and their residents, "the natives," amusing.

Because of our regular visits to both towns over a period of many years, we like to think the year-round residents accept us, but there are occasions when we catch an unguarded exchange of looks between them, and realize that after more than a quarter-century we are still on probation. These occasions are increasingly rare, for most of our acquaintances in both communities have become friends, and have learned by now that we share most of their views. In common with them we have little use for those who misuse the mountains, we frown on senseless exploitation of their resources, and we grow as bitter as the residents at visitors who leave litter-middens, hack pointlessly on the trunks of living trees, carve initials in the soft bark of aspens, and mar the faces of boulders with spray-painted graffiti.

Our reluctance to leave camp and visit these supply centers does not come from any dislike of the towns or their people. We simply feel that we should be self-sustaining and independent in our high-country camp, and by leaving it admit that we must look to others for many of our basic needs.

Actually, we enjoy the trip if it is not repeated too often; intervals of about three weeks between resupplying is our usual schedule. This is about as long as our improvised refrigeration system in the spring will keep meat fresh, even though we use first such quick-spoiling meats as pork and ground beef, and pre-cook stewing meats and roasts. The cool springwater flowing around their containers will keep partly cooked meat in good condition until we are ready to finish cooking a roast or add vegetables to our parboiled stew meat.

Friends unaccustomed to keeping house without mechanical refrigeration often question the efficiency of our springwater-chilled cooler. We tell them a Sierra story that could be either true or apochryphal, of Jim Bridger, one of the mountain men who first explored the range. On one of his trips, Bridger had a brush with a band of Ute Indians while crossing Nevada. He escaped, but with an arrow in his back, behind and below his armpit. Alone, he could not reach around to cut out the flint arrowhead, so he snapped off the shaft and went on his way. After roaming the mountains for the summer, Bridger left via the western slope and stopped in Sacramento to visit a doctor and have the embedded arrowhead removed. The doctor expressed surprise that the wound had not festered, to which Bridger replied, "Shucks, Doc, meat don't spile in them Sierra mountains."

Even in the cool high-country air, meat will spoil if left uncooked too long, but we have had good success in keeping fresh meat for as long as three weeks in our primitive refrigerator. The only spoilage we have had has been of meats that once never spoiled: cured ham and bacon. This was our introduction to modern wet-cured meats, which have little resemblance to honest smoke-cured ham and bacon. We later learned that, unless it is frozen, wet-cured meat will develop maggots even in our electric refrigerator at home. In the high country, though, there seems to be a quality of atmospheric purity that enables us to store our foods for such long periods in our makeshift cooler. Still, we don't press our luck, and when the day comes when supplies must be replenished we hike to the car and start for one of the towns.

Some sections of the unpaved roads over which our trip starts are very old indeed, a few were trails that grew into roads, trails scouted originally by the mountain men: Bridger, Jed Smith, Joe Walker, Kit Carson, Jim Beckwourth, in the early 1800s. Some of these roads run today through passes named for the trail-blazers. Other roads were hewed out by rule-of-thumb surveyors in the 1850s, when stagecoaches and wagons hauled passengers, mining equipment, ore, and bullion between the Washoe diggings in Nevada and the Mother Lode towns in California's western foothills. Loggers scratched out haulaway roads and even a few miles of rail were laid north and south for carrying logs to sawmills located on the rivers. None of the railroads lasted very long after the cross-Sierra link of the transcontinental railroad was completed and the lumber boom waned. The transcontinental railway doomed the high-country roads to disuse when it started carrying the shipments that had been handled by the ore wagons and the passengers who'd jolted on the stagecoaches.

There were no artists among the men who marked the first passes and pioneered in surveying and establishing those high-country roads that still survive, but all of them must have shared a strong artistic strain. There are few places along any of the Sierra's back roads that do not offer glimpses of peaks framed by sloping valleys, of meadows stretching green below sheer drop-offs, as the roads wind over narrow gashes sliced below the crests. These vistas could not be sheer accident; they must have been seen and planned by the men who staked out the routes the roads were to take. Or perhaps they are accidental, at that; in the high country such scenic vistas are impossible to avoid unless all roads are replaced by subways.

It may well be that we enjoy the back roads, quiet and rutted and unpaved, partly because we are aware that they cannot always stay as they are. In the high country as around the world, the cycle of change is speeding up. It was not as swift in the past, when the mountains were first settled by primitive tribes that moved into the broad sheltered valleys of the central and southern Sierra. These tribes had a flint and basket-weaving culture, their transitory occupancy of the mountain valleys did not alter their surroundings. The first modern incursions of mountain men from the east changed the slopes only slightly; they were not settlers but scouts, explorers, trappers. They denuded the country of beaver and mink and other furbearers, but could not trap all the animals. A seed stock remained after the mountain men had gone and the numbers of animals increased between their departure and the next wave of visitors.

These were the miners, pursuing the illusions of Golconda. In places where they found gold they gouged into the great flanks of the hills, washed away soft gravelled bluffs, filled streams with silt and altered their courses. The miners ravaged the surface of the mountain sides, leaving great patches of raw earth exposed, but bareness is alien to nature. Seeds dropped on the naked soil and rooted, vegetation grew, the scars were hidden as they healed.

While the miners were still at work the next wave arrived, the tree fellers, who stripped the slopes of their giant pines and rutted their sides with roads and trails. They found vistas of forests and left behind them devastations of fresh stumps; but as had the miners, the loggers moved on. Where the forests had been, the soil still held seed-studded pinecones; the seeds grew to saplings, the saplings to trees. Insects, termites and wood ants reduced the stumps to shreds and the shreds to dust, and the forests were restored.

Finally the settlers arrived. Some had come with the earlier waves and remained after the gold and trees had been taken away, and others joined them. They brought herds of cattle and flocks of sheep, and the animals crowded the meadows. The grazing beasts stripped away the grass cover and their hooves cut into the thin layer of earth, and when the rains fell and summer's return melted the snow, the water washed away the loosened meadow soil.

Within a few years it could be seen that even the massive bulk of the mountains would not sustain forever the burdens men were loading on the range. Restraints were placed on the ways the earth could be used, lumbermen limited to cutting a limited number and size of logs, herds of cattle and sheep reduced to end overgrazing, controls established over water impoundments that could alter the levels of streams and change the courses of their beds. Hunters and fishermen could no longer take so great a harvest of deer or fish, and campers were required to control their fires and to avoid spots where blazes could spread destruction.

None of these restrictions barred human use of the mountains, and in an ideal world there should be no restrictions that would do this. In practice, though, there are always a few who convert use into abuse. It would be unfortunate if the excesses of the abusers should ever result in the over-regulation of those who respect the integrity of the Sierra. At this writing the chief abusers are those whose machines, by misuse and carelessness, can potentially damage the fragile crust of earth that lies thinly over the granite bedrock. If it should be necessary to choose between machines and mountains, we would take the side of the mountains.

Before men created machines with which nature could not cope, nature had its own way of dealing with those who tried to strike into the mountains' heart. There is an example of this within a few miles of the lake, on a gently-sloping meadow where today not even shadow trails remain to mark the location of a city that sprang up overnight, mushroomed into a population of almost 4,000, then vanished as quickly as it had burgeoned. Unlike other places where cities once stood, the meadow shows no trace other than a carved marker to indicate that a town once existed there.

Ghost towns are plentiful. Though there are none in the high country, they abound in the Sierra's foothills both on the eastern and western slopes. But there is no ghost town on the meadow; there are no eroded foundations or crumbling chimneys, no vestiges of walls or basement holes where houses once stood, no squared shadows of foundation sites

nor ruts of streets. There is not even a midden-heap to attract the archaeologists of future centuries.

When we first heard of the vanished city the marker that
now marks its site had not yet been put in place. We
searched diligently, trying to find some hint, some relic,
some shard from a discarded possession, as evidence that
people had once lived there. All we ever discovered was a
warped, weathered board with three hand-wrought nails in
one squared end. The meadow looks as though it has stood
undisturbed since grass first sprouted from its soil.

Yet during the days when gold mining was breathing its
last in the Sierra high country, the vanished city occupied
this meadow. It came into being when all the big gold strikes
had been made, when no new bonanzas were being found.
By then the hardrock veins were reluctantly yielding the last
traces of their fine gold, the sands of placer works growing
barren. In the foothills to the west and the high desert to the
east, thousands of men and women who had joined the rush
to riches were shifting from one waning mining camp to
another, seeking at best stability, at worst a place where they
could scrape together food and a temporary shelter.

An illusory hope of a major new gold strike created the
city in the high-country meadow. Called Meadow City, occasionally Summit City in its first months, by the few
chroniclers who told of its life in a handful of diaries, letters
and newspaper clippings that survive after a century, the
town's location was chosen a short distance from the site of
the strike, on the main road between Virginia City in
Nevada and the Mother Lode town of Nevada City in the
foothills in California. The road ran at this place along a high
crest. It was heavily travelled during the months when it was
clear of snow; stages drawn by four-horse teams and slow ox
wagons loaded with ore, bullion and mining machinery kept
it busy. The road crossed the spine of the Sierra at Heness
Pass after climbing in switchbacks up the eastern escarpment
from Verdi, just on the California–Nevada line, then
followed the high ridges until it dipped into the Yuba River
valley to the northwest.

This stagecoach road was used until the 1880s, but it had

died as a principal artery in 1870, when the railroad line over Donner Pass came into use. Two decades later, in 1890, the first direct trans-Sierra highway was built, paralleling the rails, and stagecoaches and ore wagons quit using the steep, winding Heness Pass route. The sixty overnight stage stops, all having an office, bunkhouse, dining room, corrals and barns, that stood at five- to six-mile intervals along the old road were moved or torn down; only one still survives. The road survives in places, though where it once passed close to the lake it is reduced to a pair of almost invisible potholed ruts.

In 1863 a vein of high-yielding quartz was found in granite bedrock near the meadow where the city came to be built. Word of the strike spread from the Mother Lode to the Washoe diggings, and hard-rock miners began flocking to the site. Unlike placer mining, which calls for no skills except the ability to swing a shovel, and no equipment other than a gold pan or a wooden Long Tom washer sluice that can be whacked together in a half-hour, hard-rock operations require complex machines and substantial structures to house them and skilled men to operate them. The typical hard-rock miner was a cut above the average gold-field drifter. He was usually a Welsh- or Cornishman, a man of family and substance, accustomed to a comfortable house and a reasonably settled life. After they are proved productive, hard-rock veins normally give employment to men of this kind for many years.

Meadow City's first buildings went up as soon as the snow melt opened the stagecoach road in the summer of 1864, and by winter the town had seven stores and nearly four hundred residences. The following summer a sawmill began operating a dozen or so miles south of the townsite, near the headwaters of the Little Truckee River. It provided the material for the mine buildings and for the new homes and stores of the mushrooming city. That summer saw the number of stores increase to thirty and the four hundred dwellings multiply to twelve hundred.

On the main business street there were several two-story structures and a three-story hotel. Mineshafts had been blasted deep into the granite, new veins of gold were found with almost every blast set off. Chinese laborers, jobless because work on the railway roadbed over the Sierra hump had tapered off, were brought in to quarry stone, cut it into blocks, and build a dam at the outlet of a small lake, little better than a snowpond, that lay at one edge of the meadow. The lake was intended to provide a dependable supply of water for the stamping mill that was being built to process ore from the new mine as well as to supply the needs of the new city.

Winters had been mild in 1864 and 1865, but in 1866 the snow began falling early in September. It was not an early passing storm; the snow came down unremittingly once it began. The heavy drifts that formed were worry piled atop worry, for intensification of mining operations in the late summer had revealed that what were originally taken for rich gold veins were no more than isolated pockets. New shafts were put down in search of the veins which everyone thought must thread bountifully through the granite, but none were discovered. Work on the stamping mill stopped. The early snow, arriving just at this time, caused morale to sink still further. As the big flakes kept swirling down and the drifts piled up to the eaves of the new city's houses, a gloomy forecast ran through the town that the winter ahead would be worse than that of 1846, when the Donner party had been trapped by drifts only fifty or so miles south of where Meadow City now stood. This most gruesome of all Western experiences was still fresh in most minds in 1866.

By mid-October snow blanketed the meadow to a depth of fifteen feet. The roof trees of smaller houses were covered. Worse, the early onset of winter had given Meadow City residents no chance to lay in food. The stages and gold wagons had been halted, as had supply wagons, by the first week's drifts. The only new faces to be seen in the town were those of a handful of intrepid foot-travellers using snowshoes to cross the mountains. These brought dismal word of winter's severity in places other than the meadow where the newborn city stood.

Late in November there occurred a phenomenon rare

indeed at the city's 7,000-foot altitude. A sudden thaw melted the snow until bare ground showed in many places. The thaw made the stagecoach road passable, though not by wheeled vehicles. The panic that had been building found its outlet; most of the four thousand inhabitants of Meadow City left, abandoning anything they could not carry in backpacks. Furnishings were left in houses, bread left in ovens that grew cold, and in some homes tables set for meals that would never be served were left untouched. The exodus was not total, about two hundred people stayed, most of them merchants who had invested a lifetime of savings in their new stores and stock. The mine operators and a few stubborn miners also remained behind.

November's thaw held out a promise that December did not fulfill. Before the first day of 1867, the city's single-storied houses were all buried under snowdrifts thirty to forty feet high. Those few who had stayed dug tunnels to connect the inhabited structures and survived by pooling food left by the departed residents and by burning furniture for firewood after all the laid-by pine chunks were gone. A handful of the thousands who had retreated from the winter came back with the return of summer weather, but their chief purpose was to salvage what they could from the possessions they had left behind. Some did remain, and efforts were made to reopen the mines, but it was a losing proposition from the first try. Snow-melt water in quantities unforeseen flowed into many shafts; those that could be worked yielded ore of such low grade that the attempts soon stopped.

Before the summer of 1867 had ended, Meadow City's life was over. The heavy, unusually wet snow melted slowly, its water turned the meadow into a quagmire, the roads into rivers. Even at midsummer, supplies could be brought in only by pack animals, for wagons bogged to their beds in the muddy ruts that remained as roads. The only way to travel was by horseback, muleback, or on foot. People started to go, anxious to escape another winter, and before the first snow the exodus was almost complete. An early snow flurry finished it; the handful who had stayed joined the trek downslope. Once more, houses, furniture, all but the most treasured and most portable personal possessions were left behind.

Snowshoe Thompson, the incredible winter mail carrier of the Sierra, who traversed the range from east to west and back several times each winter on a pair of homemade skis—"Norwegian snowshoes" these were called, then—passed through Meadow City in the late winter of 1867. History fails to note why Thompson detoured from his usual more southerly route; perhaps it was his perfectly human curiosity to take a look at the abandoned town. He skiied along the abandoned Main Street between parallel rows of chimneys sticking up above the snow, which was so deep that Thompson had to kneel to look in the second-floor windows of the big deserted hotel.

He described the scene for a reporter from the *Sacramento Union* when he reached California, and allowing for reportorial license of the period Thompson's description paints a vivid picture. "Beds were made," he said. "Night-stands stood by them, washbowls and pitchers on the stands and towels on the racks. It was as though the room was ready to greet some tired guest who never would arrive."

In 1868 one courageous man returned to Meadow City. His name was Henry Hartley, and he lived there until his death in the late 1890s, still predicting that the town would be reborn. It was not, of course. The buildings grew more weatherbeaten each year, were dismantled gradually, a board or two at a time "borrowed" by a prospector who wanted to build himself a shack, or by a rancher who needed lumber for a sheepherder's shanty. Homesteaders, beginning now to settle in the high country, mined the deserted houses of their furniture, ripped out walls to provide lumber for their new homes, and carted away the chimneys brick by brick.

In 1903 a utility company bought the meadow with its lake as part of an expansion of its hydroelectric power generating facilities. The dam the Chinese had built was raised to impound more water, but no generating plant was located there; instead, a sluice was constructed to drain the water to plants downslope. What was left of Meadow City's buildings went into equipment sheds, crew bunkhouses, forms for concrete. Construction completed, the contractors hauled away the materials to be used elsewhere and cleared the meadow of any residues of houses or buildings. Thus, in spite of several searches we have made of the city's site, the only evidence we ever found that Meadow City had indeed existed was that piece of warped board sawed square at one end, containing three bent nails.

A half-dozen miles from the site of Meadow City we did find a visible reminder of the pioneers who came early to the Sierra. Our discovery was made just off a trail that follows the wide crest of a ridge rising above the steep-sloped walls of the valley beyond the lake's basin. The trail starts from nowhere and ends nowhere. At some time there must have been points at which it began and ended, but we have walked the full length of its visible traces several times without finding any clues to its original purpose. The trail is simply there, along the crest, two or three miles of a well-defined pathway that ends at a sheer cliff at one end and fades into nothingness at the other.

It is not a deer trail or animal path; though it is now used by animals, we are familiar enough with forest signs to tell the difference in trail origins. The trail was created by men, but there are no others nearby, no roads within a dozen miles, no remainders of logging or gold exploration or any other human activity. After it fades away, the trail does not show up again. From all indications, an old slide cut off its other end, and the clue to its origin may have been wiped out by this earth movement. We have searched at both ends without result. There is simply no extension of the trail at either of them.

At about the midpoint of what is left of the path, a tiny stream, small enough to be spanned by two spread hands, trickles across it. Thinking the stream's course might give us a clue to the trail's use, we followed it to the point where it originates in a bubbling spring high on the slope that rises on one side of the ridge. Water from the spring is live on the tongue; it has in its tang the essence of the always-cold Sierra deeps. We ate lunch by the spring, and drank from it, then began rambling around the clearing in which the spring rose from a rock cleft.

At first we saw nothing to distinguish the clearing from a hundred others where we've paused to eat or rest in our walks. We were thinking of returning to the trail when we stumbled over the rough rectangle of stones, half-buried under the duff, shrouded from our notice by scattered pine-cones and broken branches. The rectangle was imperfect and broken, with many of its stones missing, but enough of it was left to show that it was obviously an arrangement made by human hands, and its size and shape left no doubt that the stones had been placed to outline a grave.

At first we did not see what remained of the marker lying at the base of a tree trunk near one end of the stone rectangle. When we picked it up and brushed away the forest detritus that had half-buried it, we were holding a weathered board, one end split away, on which the initials "J. T. W." were carved. Below the letters were two numbers and part of a third, which could only have been a date, "18– –." We examined the board closely. The initials were clear and deeply incised, but the missing portion of the board had split away through the third digit of the date numbers and removed the fourth completely. From the shape of the portion of the third number that remained, it could equally well have been 3, 5, 6, 8, 9, or 0.

Inside the rectangle of stones the ground had sagged a bit, as is common with old graves in which uncoffined bodies or those in wooden caskets were buried. In time, as earth reclaims its own, the surface above such bodies sinks a trifle. Wordlessly, we began to search for the missing portion of the marker, but could not find it. There were a few splinters of wood close to the spot where the marker had been lying, but we could not fit them together or determine whether any of the shreds bore traces of carving.

Our emotions had been stirred almost from the moment we realized what we had found. Without consulting one another or discussing it, we began gathering stones and re-shaping the rectangle around the sagging soil. Some of the stones we picked up were near enough to the grave to have

From the moment we realized what we had found, we began gathering stones and reshaping the rectangle around the sagging soil.

formed part of its original outline. A few fitted into the depressions where they had once rested. Later, we came back with nails and a hatchet and replaced the remaining section of the marker on the bole of the tree from which it had fallen. We found traces of the wooden pegs by which it had originally been fixed to the tree trunk, and which had rotted away in the course of the years.

Our later speculations over the grave have led us to some deductions that seem logical, though necessarily inconclusive and unprovable. Whoever he was, J. T. W. could not have been a permanent resident of the high country, or his grave would have been near a house or settlement or an old timber stand or mine, and we found no sign that there had ever been a dwelling or any other work of men in the vicinity.

We decided that the year of his death could not have been 180–, for the first trappers and scouts did not come into the Sierra until about 1824; if the date was originally carved in 183–, or even as early as 182–, he might have been a trapper or roving mountain man. If the lost date was 185– or 186–, he would more likely have been a prospector or lumber worker, or even one of a crew surveying possible routes for the trans-Sierra railroad line. The chance that he was one of an emigrant party from the east is very slight, for their wagons crossed the range much further north or south than the place where he was buried. We could never deduce with any certainty what J. T. W.'s mission in the high country might have been if the date was 188– or 189–.

One or two lurid conclusions did surface, but we discarded them as unlikely. Among these was the possibility that J. T. W. might have been a member of an outlaw gang seeking to escape from pursuit, perhaps wounded in the foothills of the Mother Lode country to the west, or the rough mining camps in Nevada to the east. We did not think this likely, though obviously J. T. W. had not been travelling alone. If his companions had been outlaws, they would probably not have taken time to mark the grave with stones and a carved headboard.

We believe that J. T. W. must have been held in great esteem by his companion or companions. They went beyond the simple duty of digging and filling his grave; they placed stones to outline it and carved a tablet to go above it. The carving was crude; it must have been done with a hunting knife or jackknife, and we thought, though could not be sure, that we could detect traces of charring in the letters, as though the marker's maker had tried to deepen them and make them stand out more clearly by tracing them with a burning twig after incising them. The board was so cracked and weathered that it was hard to tell if this had been done.

Many things might have caused J. T. W.'s death. A more complete date might have provided a clue. For instance, if the month had been included we might have guessed that a winter storm had resulted in pneumonia, fatal during that period. Appendicitis, a fall, a bolting horse, the dropping of a widowmaker limb from one of the pines; any of these might have been fatal. Odds favor a natural illness or accident, for the high country has seen little violence; the bloodshed of Gold Rush days was confined to the foothills. Even the grisly story of the Donners was not one of violence, but one of misery and desperation.

There were no hostile Indians in the high country, though J. T. W. might have been wounded by the Utes or Paiutes as he crossed Nevada. No outlaw gangs operated in the high country at any time, and the burial site is far removed from any regular outlaw trails. Though the odds are against it, J. T. W. might have been killed by a grizzly, for these huge hostile bears were common in the Sierra until the early 1900s, and were noted as being the only animals in the range that would attack humans unprovoked.

In spite of our speculations, we still know nothing of J. T. W., of his reasons for being in the mountains, or the cause and date of his death, but we still feel an obligation to the unknown man or woman—the former much more likely than the latter—who lies in the grave. At least once during our summer in camp we visit the grave, make sure the marker is still on the tree, the stones still in place around it. We hope that when we no longer come to the pine grove someone else will have discovered the spot, and will carry on with the small maintenance chores we have chosen to undertake.

If there is someone who does this in future years, we are sure he will feel, as we have come to feel, a kinship with the unknown J. T. W. The spot where his body lies is one that might have been selected by anybody who loves ·the high country: a quiet pine grove on a secluded ridge. There, the summer sun falls through shifting shadows cast by tall green trees. The pines blunt the fury of the winter storms. On all sides below the ridge the land lies revealed, a sweeping vista of valleys, the occasional glint of water from a lake or stream, and beyond all, the shimmering distant peaks thrusting into the sky. Implicit in the blue of the sky and the lakes, the dark green of the pines, and the emerald meadows visible from the crest is the promise that the mountains will live on.

B THE EAVER

W ithin three miles of the lake there is a large beaver colony. It has not been there long; having been exceedingly rare in the high country for nearly a century, beavers have come back, and their dams are seen on many streams between the 6,000- and 7,500-foot levels. In this case, man instead of nature deserves credit for restoring a species to an area from which it had almost vanished.

Often while camping at the lake we have hiked to another even more isolated lake, smaller and at a higher altitude, too far from any road to be considered for a camp that would need to be resupplied. But this small lake is attractive, is stocked with brook trout, and has become one of our favorite destinations for hikes. The way leads past the spot where the beaver colony now lives. For the high country it is an easy walk, requiring no real climbing. We stroll down the slope to the long valley and then make a slow pull up its far wall to the ridge where the second lake lies. There is no trail except the vague traces we have left ourselves, but we know the easiest grades by now, and the places where the ground is softest underfoot. We walk through pleasant stands of sun-dappled pines on the slopes, and whispering, dancing groves of aspen on the valley floor.

One year as we crossed the valley we found it had changed. Where there had been a large mountain meadow with a saucy little creek tumbling through it we encountered a big expanse of marshy bog surrounding a calm pond. At first we took it for a snowpond, but one had never been there before. Then we thought that since we had not visited the small lake the year before, we might have forgotten the way, though we were sure we'd followed familiar landmarks on our way down into the valley. But when we looked more closely at the banks of the pond, we saw the toppled aspens and straggly willows that mark all beaver workings.

When beavers colonize a spot and build a dam in a place

where soft-bark trees mingle with pines, they invariably pass up the pine trees. Here, they had cut down about half of the three or four dozen aspens that had shared the meadow-edge with thick-trunked Jeffreys, and the clean white of point-topped aspen stumps told us that this was an active colony. We walked around the pond, skirting the boggy stretch that bordered it, to inspect the dam. It was early morning, and as beavers do not often work by daylight, there was no danger that we would disturb the colonists.

Judging by the size of the dam and the pond it backed up, the colony was small; our guess was that its population was only two or three pairs. At its top the dam spanned fifteen to eighteen feet, and the pond covered barely two acres of meadow. We picked our way across the bog to the dam on hummocks of grass and stood on the edge where it touched land. We could see now that the pond was quite shallow, not more than three or four feet deep at the dam's center. Until then we'd never examined closely a beaver dam located in the mountains. Most of those we'd inspected were in California's San Joaquin and Sacramento valleys, where the beaver were reclaiming land ruined by gold dredges; these dams were invariably very narrow and the water behind them quite deep.

We had heard from some forgotten source that beaver in the mountains seldom build lodges in their ponds, but follow the habit of their close relatives the big rodents called *Aplodontia*, or mountain beaver, which live in burrows around the pond's edge, with entrance tunnels under the waterline. The entrances slant upward from their opening and at some point before reaching the den describe a curve similar to those found in plumbing drains, to keep rising water from flooding the beavers' homes.

We also knew enough about beavers' general habits to realize that the animals would not leave their burrows before dark. We went on to the small lake, resolving to come back some evening and watch the beaver at work. This was an opportunity we did not have for three years during which business activities made it impossible for us to spend more than an occasional long weekend at the lake. One year we did take time to visit the pond; we found that it had grown into a complex of three dams and as many ponds, proof that the colony was flourishing. Our curiosity was unsatisfied, so we spent some time tracing the history of beaver in the Sierra.

Beaver pelts lured the first white men into the mountains. By 1820 the trapping mountain men had almost wiped out beaver in the northern Rockies and had moved as far west as the Columbia River watershed, following the route explored by Lewis and Clark. From the Columbia they trapped south through the Cascades, but never found areas as rich in beaver as those they had cleared out. The northern Sierra was no more productive, but the demand for furs was still great and the trappers persisted. They continued to push south, taking not only beaver but mink and marten as well. South of the Kern River headwaters the animals were so scarce that the trigger-tempered mountain men gave up in disgust and returned north. For perhaps ten years they made their sets in the high country, until they had cleared most of the beaver ponds of their builders.

In the mid-1830s the market for beaver pelts withered away; silk was replacing beaver fur as the material preferred by gentlemen of fashion for their tophats. The styles for women's coats had also changed; seal and sable had become the fashion, beaver, mink and marten were passé. The trappers hauled out of the Sierra and for two decades the fur-bearers lived unmolested; their numbers were restored. Then the gold miners arrived and did a more thorough job of wiping out the beaver than had the mountain men with their steel traps.

Placer mining was always the chief method used to extract gold from the Mother Lode, and when the solitary prospectors had cleared out the river-bed pockets, the search moved to the gravelled sides of the foothills. Hand extraction was too slow. Big hoses were brought in to send jets of water against the hillsides and bluffs, washing them away. The loose mud was channeled into sluices with corrugated bottoms that trapped the heavy flakes of gold settling out of the slushy flow.

Hoses soon gave way to "monitors"—cannon-sized nozzles mounted on strong movable platforms. These sent a ten-inch stream of water at high velocity onto the gravel-studded hillsides and washed them away much more efficiently. This kind of mining demanded huge amounts of water. To secure a supply, crews were sent to the high country to build sluices or flumes, and when natural fall proved insufficient, streams were dammed to create reservoirs. The outlets ran from the 6,000- to 7,000-foot levels in open wooden troughs or flumes, and reached the mining areas at 3,500 to 4,000 feet with enough pressure to make the monitors effective.

Beavers became the enemies of placer miners, though no enmity was displayed by the animals. Beaver dams occupied most of the best natural dam-sites. When the mining crews destroyed the beaver dams the beavers rebuilt them using the legs of the flumes, which they gnawed through as they would have gnawed trees. Professional riflemen were hired by the mining companies to protect the flumes. The beavers were not merely dispossessed, but were shot and tossed aside like carrion. Beaver pelts still had no value, so the shooters seldom took time to skin them. At that place and in that time, small value was placed on any sort of wildlife.

In the high country and in the foothills the beaver were almost wiped out. A few did escape, and migrated to the valleys. They arrived just in time to meet a new army of enemies, the farmers, who by then were beginning to build irrigation ditches to bring water to their crops. Beavers followed their instincts and dammed up the ditches, often gnawing down fruit trees from adjoining orchards to get the materials for their dams. The farmers killed beavers as indiscriminately as had the miners. Again, some of the animals escaped and took refuge in the towering rock windrows that stood on land despoiled by gold dredges.

These monstrous machines had begun devouring California's central valleys after the placer gold ran out. Powerful motors were mounted on shallow-draft barges that would float in a few inches of water; the motors powered toothed buckets or scoops fixed to endless belts that passed along swivelled booms protruding in front of the barge. The buckets stripped away soil to a depth of fifteen feet, dumped earth and stones and small boulders on a moving screen sprayed by jets of water, which washed the loose soil down into corrugated troughs where the gold settled and collected.

Moving in straight parallel lines, the dredges dumped the rock and mud off on one side of their paths as they inched along. The rocks formed twenty-foot-high windrows, leaving the land covered with a series of furrows, the once-fertile earth washed under the ridges of rocks. A gold dredge showed a profit if it extracted as little as a half-ounce of gold dust from every ton of earth and stones it moved. Until their operation was halted, belatedly, in the late 1940s, the dredges had turned hundreds of square miles of formerly fertile soil into a lunar-like landscape.

Into these desolate, ruined furrows the beavers moved, looking for a place safe from enemies. They built dams in the few inches of water that ran at the bottoms of some of the furrows, using willows that they often had to drag for a mile or two across the ridges. But even in this ruined and rocky desolation the beavers flourished. Their colonies grew and multiplied and their dams seeded willows in cracks where wind-blown dust created little pockets of soil between the stones. Islands of green began to show amid the rocks.

Then styles changed again, and beaver fur came back into fashion. The beaver ponds attracted trappers, and by the late 1930s the animals had again been so severely decimated that they were put under the protection of California's game laws. Trapping was stopped, and the beavers once more began to multiply. They became so numerous that they began to migrate from their rocky shelters. They built dams across irrigation ditches, flooded farm fields and gnawed down orchards again. Farmers began shooting beavers in spite of laws protecting them. To quiet complaints, the state game department decided to move the beavers back to the high country. Later we learned that a single pair dropped on the meadow in the valley near the lake had started the colony we encountered.

During the three years between the time we first stumbled on the beaver dam and the time when we could resume our summer-long camps at the lake, the colony multiplied. On our second visit there had been three dams; when we saw the ponds a third time, the three had become six, two upstream from the original three and downstream from the single dam we first found. The meadow had become a series of shimmering quiet ponds, its aspect changed completely. Before the beaver came, the narrow shallow creek had flowed between low banks dotted scantily with thin stands of willows, across a flat barely covered with coarse squawgrass and bordered by aspens mingled with a few Jeffrey pines. The granite bedrock had broken bare through the thin soil and protruded grey above the grass tops. The ground underfoot had been hard, the grass clumps hiding a scattering of sharp stones.

Seepage from the beaver ponds had now softened the soil, and grasses mingled with cinquefoil grew thickly between ponds and trees. Willows taller than a man's head flourished around the ponds, their spindly shoots encouraged to grow high because the beaver kept the clumps thinned by constant pruning of the lowest, smallest, tenderest growth. There were far more willow clumps around the edges of the ponds than had ever grown by the creek. On the meadow's margin fewer aspens stood, and the point-tipped stumps of trees now gone showed how the beaver had increased their activity as the colony had grown in numbers. Here and there a big aspen trunk slanted along the ground, stripped of top, branches and bark.

It was impossible to get near the original dam, which now extended forty feet or so in length, because of the ponds backed up by the new downstream dams. There were still no lodges in the ponds, but when we walked upstream parallel to the creekbed we could see through the clear still water and make out the dark blotches that marked the underwater burrow entrances.

Inspection of the smallest downstream dam and its buttresses showed that by instinct beaver build much as would a school-trained engineer. The base of the dam was made from heavy sections of tree trunks with large branch-stubs left on them; the trunks had been dragged into position at an angle to the current's flow and held in place by stones and mud. Intertwined with the foundation trunks were small branches and twigs. The construction looked haphazard at first glance, but study showed its logic: a heavy fixed base that held a buttress of interlaced material designed to slow down rather than stop the water's flow.

A trained engineer would have called the dam incomplete or unfinished, because it leaked small trickles of water at a dozen or more places on its downstream face. This human engineer would have criticized the work for its raw look, for it was anything but neat. The materials of which it was composed were not arranged in neat courses, but placed only where they were needed to hold the brushy body of the dam together. There was no denying its functional ability, though. It was a classic example of the architectural dictum that function dictates design. The dam did the job for which it had been built, maintaining a constant level of water in the pond and letting enough water trickle through to keep the pressure of that impounded from washing out the structure.

While we inspected the dam, the sun went down. We had come prepared for an all-night vigil. Making a wide detour around the muddy area adjoining the colony's ponds, we gathered up the sandwiches and thermos jug of coffee that we had left with our blankets and groundcloth at the edge of the meadow, then settled down at the base of one of the big Jeffrey pines to wait for darkness and for the early-rising full moon.

When there are no artificial lights to dazzle and the transition from daylight to nightfall can be made as nature intended, human eyes adjust easily and automatically to night vision. We were about thirty yards from the nearest beaver pond, but in the brightness after moonrise the ripple on its glassy surface was easily seen when the first beaver broke water a few feet from the bank. We could see its stubby wide head at the tip of the vee it cut as it swam to shore and crawled out. Moonlight danced off droplets as the animal shook its chunky body to get rid of the water clinging to its fur. The beaver reared up, bracing itself with its tail, and sat erect for a few moments while it turned and swivelled,

inspecting the pond and the shore line. Apparently, the
animal was the scout for the colony, and it must have transmitted an "all clear" message by some unnoticed, un-
fathomed animal sense, for soon after its inspection ended
the heads of several more beaver broke water.

It was difficult to count them at first, for they milled
around the pond for a short while, some diving intermittently, others coming to shore to join the one that had emerged
first. At last all of the swimmers climbed up to the bank on
their stubby legs and we counted eight of them. Their fur
looked like nothing that would be a trapper's prize, for it
stuck out in straggly tufts all over their sturdy rounded
bodies. When they had all gathered on the bank they moved
very little, but sat chittering in high-pitched tones, looking
for all the world like senior club members at a committee
meeting.

Even the most skeptical zoographers now reluctantly admit that most animals have some form of communication
among themselves and that in some this facility has reached a
high stage of development. It was quite apparent that the
beaver on the bank were communicating with one another.
Within a few minutes they had reached a consensus, and the
convocation broke up. The animals slid into the water. Three
of them swam toward the dam, the others moved up the
pond, and we lost sight of them in the shadows the pines cast
over the water.

Obviously an allocation of work had been made during the
time the beavers sat chittering on the bank. The three that
swam to the dam divided up when they reached it. One
crawled up to the top of the structure, the others began diving along its upstream side. The beaver atop the dam
scuttled back and forth over the matted branches, stopping
now and then at a protruding stub to shake one of the
branches with its forepaws. It must have found one that was
loose and needed reinforcing, for when one of the animals in
the water came to the surface the beaver on the dam
squeaked a few high-pitched tones and the second one
crawled up on the dam.

Together the two beavers shook and pulled vigorously at

one of the branches sticking up from the dam's upstream side. In a moment, one of them began to paw at the point where the branch emerged from the tangled, uneven top. The other dived into the pond and swam to the willows on the far shore. It disappeared into a willow clump and we could see the tops of the thicket shaking. The beaver came out, dragging a sturdy willow branch, and towed it to the dam.

By this time the third beaver had emerged from the water and was on top of the dam. The second beaver arrived with the willow shoot, and the three of them hauled it from the water. They began prodding the butt of the willow into the dam, pushing and levering it, to work it into the crude latticework. One dived, presumably to guide the branch from below the surface. It stayed underwater for what seemed to us a long while, but must have been a quite normal submersion for a beaver. Finally it joined the other two on the dam. They sat for a short while in silence, then all three slid off the dam and vanished in the pond.

They did not emerge, and for an hour or so there was no activity within our light-limited range of view. The surface of the beaver pond settled down into a series of long recurring swells with softly rounded crests that caught and threw back silver highlights from the full moon that by this time was crossing the sky and beginning to dip toward the treetops across the pond from us. We waited, swaddled in blankets against the chill that had come with deep night, ate our sandwiches, sipped hot coffee, and listened to the night voices of the forest.

We'd almost concluded that there would be no more signs of beaver that night when we saw a broad vee of ripples spreading across the wide swathe of light cast on its surface by the descending moon. A large aspen branch, fully leafed, was floating toward the dam. Another look showed us the spatulate head of the beaver that was towing the branch; then in the ripples behind it, we saw another beaver, and still another, towing more branches. We assumed these were the animals that had left earlier.

On the far side of the pond the beavers hauled the

branches up a sloping stretch of bank. The area was in deep shade and hard to see; the moon was behind the tree tops and the bank was a dappled mixture of brightly lighted and totally dark patches. We could see the beaver only intermittently, but the rasping of their teeth was loud in the otherwise still night; we guessed that they were cutting up the branches. Our guess was confirmed when they began pulling leafed twigs and short pieces of the limbs into the pond and diving with them to the bottom. We had learned enough about beaver habits to know they must be shoving into the mud the cut sections to be used as food during the winter.

This job lasted as long as we were able to see the beavers' work crew. The light was going fast, the moon had dropped behind the pines and the entire surface of the pond was in deep shadow. From our vantage point we could see only dim outlines of moving forms and the ripples on the water's dark surface as the animals made their trips between the pond and its far shore. Their gnawing went on long after darkness hid the scene. We could not tell how many beavers were at work, whether those that had worked on the dam earlier were with them, or whether their task had been only to handle the repair work. We half guessed that there might have been some division of labor of this sort, with one group responsible for gathering winter food, the other for maintenance work.

Midnight had passed by the time the sounds of the working beaver died away. The air had grown cold indeed, and we pulled our blankets up more snugly around our shoulders. Leaning back against the bole of the pine tree, we relaxed and dozed fitfully until the sky was bright enough for us to see the way back to camp. By then the beaver ponds were deserted, placid pools, their waters grey in the predawn light, their smooth surfaces glassy and unruffled.

N^{THE}IGHT HUNTERS

On the meadows near the lake, in the pine forest around it, on the high ridges that rise above it, night hunters prowl during the brief weeks of summer. Casual visitors to the Sierra seldom see these animals; during some summers even those familiar with the animals' haunts and habits fare little better. We glimpse the night prowlers now and then, most often as shadows moving across the meadow or lurking between meadow and trees or as dark shapes gliding on bright nights across moon-bright patches of duff between the pines, or as silhouettes in the tree branches at dusk or dawn.

During daylight hours we may on rare occasions see a badger or marten or mink abroad. Even more rarely we glimpse a coyote slinking across the bare granite of one of the ridges, moving from covert to covert. The fisher seldom goes out by day, and trapping has reduced the always-limited number of fishers in the high country to a token few hundred. A handful of wolverines, probably no more than a score or so in the entire Sierra range, survive at high altitudes, but for so many years it was the custom of hunters to shoot wolverines on sight that very, very few are left. We have never seen one, though once we found wolverine tracks on a patch of earth when we went up the high ridges beyond camp.

With more and more people penetrating the range each summer, the night hunters are moving to the most isolated, hard-to-reach places. In the matrices we prepare on little-used trails we see their pawprints with reasonable regularity, so we know they are still in residence. Coyote and marten droppings are fairly common; we see these more often than we do their tracks. Mink and badgers both bury their feces, so we can't judge how they are faring.

Porcupines are another matter. They move by day as well as by night, quite possibly because their vision is so dim that the degree of light available is unimportant to them. What

Their very short legs and feet that slant inward, under their bodies, make porcupine slow walkers but excellent climbers. They feel quite at home among the branches.

porkies lack in vision, they make up for in keenness of scent and hearing; they also have an unusual and perhaps unique sensory area in their wide spiny tails. Both people and animals are sometimes surprised, and pained at the same time, to learn this. The porcupine's tail is really its chief weapon, though it has sharp claws and teeth.

When surprised or alarmed by an alien sound or odor, a porky at once turns its back in the direction from which the alarming signal has come and starts to swing its tail slowly from side to side. If the noise or smell gets too close, it begins to flick its tail, which sometimes causes a quill or two to be dislodged and is responsible for the old belief that porkies "shoot" their quills for a distance. The tail quills may travel a foot or two when the tail is flicked, but seldom further. The action is not purposeful, but an accident of nature.

When it is brought into use as a weapon, the porcupine's tail is hypersensitive to the proximity of any threatening object. The object may be a bobcat's paw or a human hand, even a stick. Naturalists have noted the phenomenon, but have not yet succeeded in determining whether there are nerves or sensory organs in the tail that respond to heat or air currents or vibration. Whatever the medium, porcupines can sense the proximity of an object nearing them and bring up their tail to slap it before it makes contact with their body.

On our hikes we have seen the pugmarks of limping bobcats with the lines of porcupine quills under the paws. We have come across the carcasses of coyotes, with mouths so full of quills that they had starved, unable to hunt or to chew. Veterinarians have often had the same dog brought in time after time by its owner, the dog's mouth bristling with quills that had to be pulled out. Like dogs, coyotes seem unable to resist the temptation of trying to sample porky's fat, resin-flavored flesh. The temptation is generally fatal to coyotes, who have no owners to attend to having the quills removed.

There is no aggressiveness in the makeup of porcupines. They never attack, but are quite ready to defend themselves from the only wild animals that try to make a meal of them: bobcats, cougars and coyotes. The big cats will—or so legends go—occasionally succeed in flipping the porky on its back, where it can use its tail to a very limited extent in self-defense, and attack its quill-free underparts. While many improbable things are possible among animals, my inclination is to class this as pure legend. Cougars may wave a paw

at a porky, but we've never seen a cougar's pawprints show-
ing the pads filled with quills.

When we first began to look on the Sierra high country as
a living nature library as well as an attractive and satisfying
summer vacation spot, we heard many more porcupines than
we ever saw. We associated the drawling grunt with an
animal, but weren't quite sure which animal. Nor did we
think to look *up* for the source of the grunts. We then
shared the common misconception that porcupines were
slow-moving earthbound creatures. Slow-moving they are,
but they are anything but earthbound; in fact porkies are
much more at ease in trees than on the ground. They have
very short legs and feet that slant inward, under their bodies,
which makes them slow walkers but excellent climbers. They
are not nimble, like chipmunks or chickarees, but they as-
cend trees rapidly and feel quite at home among the
branches.

Especially during the early days of summer, when the pine
buds are just beginning to sprout and have not yet begun to
take on their later cone configuration, porcupines should be
looked for in trees. Porky's sensitive nose guides it to a tree
thick with buds; it clambers rapidly up the trunk until it
reaches the topmost limbs, then crawls out on a branch until
it arrives at a crotch in which it can wedge its chunky body
comfortably. Then it begins eating. Invariably, the porcupine
will select a crotch that has enough small branches and twigs
within reach to give it a long meal. From its wedged-in position the porcupine reaches out to grasp each branch in turn,
pulling it close to nip off the new buds; only when the buds
have disappeared does it let the branch spring free, and
reach at once for the next.

While it dines, the porcupine grunts, a short semi-baritone
"whuff," between swallows. Now and again it will grunt
while pulling toward itself an especially succulent-looking
load of buds. The porky may stay in a single tree for an entire afternoon, moving from one crotch to another, before its
appetite is satisfied. Then, it backs slowly down the bole,
feeling its way with its tail. If the porky happens into a stand

of seedlings or saplings, it has found the equivalent of porcupine heaven, and will go from sprouting tree to tree, denuding each one of buds, climbing any sapling that is too large to be bent down. Trees topped by porcupines when saplings frequently grow twin tips; when mature they are reminders that when very young they provided part of a porky's meal.

Although we admire the porcupine for its peaceful nature and its ability to ignore danger until danger gets within inches of its tail, we deplore the salt-hunger all porkies have. Nearly all woods dwellers share this need for salt, and apparently require more than the high-country vegetation can supply in their diets. This may reflect ancestral patterns, for most of the Sierra animals migrated from the valleys where the hot sun evaporates standing water and forms salt beds. But while most vegetarian animals crave salt, the porcupine carries to an extreme its method of satisfying the craving. If porcupines are in the neighborhood, no ax handle, no fishing rod grip, no tool or object handled by perspiring hands is safe from its teeth. Porky's sharp incisors, designed to gnaw wood, can reduce the handle of an axe or shovel to splinters in a few minutes—and will if the tool is left outside where it can be reached.

Although less inclined than porcupines to roam by day, badgers now and then make daytime visits to the meadow beyond the lake, looking for a meal of ground squirrel or gopher. Badgers are inclined to be intolerant of humans who interrupt their hunting or who arrive on the scene when they are busy digging into the burrow of one of the small vegetarians on which they feed. The badger will not retreat at once from an approaching person, but breaks its habitual silence with a gurgling hiss that grows into a full-scale growl. If the person does not go away, the badger does, scurrying off with a flurry of disgusted grunts. When encountered on a trail, or sniffing across a meadow trying to scent the underground nest of pocket gopher or ground squirrel, the badger seldom hisses or growls, but marches away with dignity on its truncated legs. We do not often see badgers, though their pawprints are much in evidence as proof of their nighttime prowlings. So are the heaps of earth on the meadow where they have clawed into a burrow looking for a midnight snack.

Anything more than a quick passing glimpse of the feral night hunters is rare. To see them properly requires a type of vision human eyes lack, but one with which the nocturnals are equipped. Lining the eyeballs of a majority of night-moving animals is a layer of membranous tissue absent from human eyes. This extra layer is photoluminescent; it catches and amplifies any light-formed image striking it and focuses this image on the retina with many times the clarity that the same image in the same light would be projected through the pupil of a human eye.

This photoluminescent layer is the same one that reflects light outward through the animal's pupil when its eyes catch the glare of a campfire or flashlight or automobile headlights. The reflection is thrown back as green or red, according to the animal's species. The color reflected from the eyes of most cats and canines is green; so is that from the larger herbivores such as deer. In the smaller species the color varies between green and red. Poachers who spotlight deer at night take advantage of this characteristic to make their illegal activities easier.

In addition to the light-amplifying membrane, animals' eyes have proportionately greater pupils than do those of humans. Especially in small creatures, the ratio of eye size to head and body size is much larger than in people. The white tissue called sclera that surrounds pupil and cornea and is so prominent in human eyes is only a thin line in most animals' eyes, and may be hidden entirely by the eyelids. Naturalists who have made scholarly studies of such things tell us that for human eyes to attain night vision equivalent to that of night-moving animals, our eyes would have to be four to six inches in diameter.

This eye formation is more noticeable on small night-moving animals than on the bigger ones; the large beasts are more likely to spend a part of their time rambling during daylight. It's especially noticeable on the burrowers and on night prowlers such as mink and marten. These two do very little daytime hunting during the weeks of summer, but they do begin moving earlier than most of the nocturnals and stay abroad later in the mornings. At these times of half-light, they generally remain in the cover of the pine groves, saving the meadows for total darkness.

If they can be judged by their hunting patterns, martens have a strong sense of family responsibility. For the first weeks of summer, before the snow has vanished and while their young are too small to come out of their dens, martens hunt singly, one always remaining behind to guard the kits. After a time of growth, the family hunts as a group, the babies learning from their parents by example and observation. Finally, after midsummer, when the young kits have matured enough to strike out for themselves, the marten pair leave the young in possession of the nest and make another for themselves. During the winter the marten mates hunt as a pair, until the birth of new kits brings back a return to the alternation between hunting and baby-sitting.

Now and again during the long twilights that mark the summer season's brief heart, we get glimpses of martens, singles as well as families, in the pine forest that extends from one shore of the lake. Except for.their small pointed heads and long bushy tails, we might be looking at a family of house cats. There is the same chasing play by the young, watched by their parents, and the squabbles that erupt among the kits are broken up by the elders. Indeed, more than other small predatory mammals, the marten most closely resembles the domestic cat in looks, actions and habits. We would like to see them more often instead of having to settle for fleeting glimpses of their rust-brown furred bodies silhouetted in the shadowed pines at dusk or dawn. We see just enough to interest us in seeing more.

In drawing a comparison between martens and domestic cats we have not overlooked the now almost legendary Sierra ringtail. The ringtail is not really an animal of the high country, though one will stray occasionally up to the 6,000- to 7,000-foot altitude. We have seen none around the lake, and only two in the valley beyond it. Very few remain now, even in the foothills where they were once numerous. Ringtails are related to the raccoon, and early miners found them easy to tame and quite adaptable to civilization; they were so common in the gold camps that they got the nickname "miner's cats." It may well be that the ringtail became so dependent on men's handouts that they lost the ability to survive in the wild. There are not many left, and inevitably the day will come when they will join the grizzly bear and timber wolf in whatever Arcady is reserved for extinct animal species.

Mink, smaller than any Sierran predator except the weasel, came very close to vanishing; at one time they were as scarce as the ringtail is today. Like the beaver, mink were almost wiped out by trappers in the days before mink farms made it easier to breed than take them in the wild. Not until the middle 1930s was any limitation put on the number of mink a trapper could take, but at that time both a bag limit and a short season were set on trapping, so now the mink are coming back. In the wild, mink have a very low survival rate; of a litter of eight, only two or three will live to maturity. Reproduction and the take of trappers now just about balance, with reproduction holding a thin lead.

Only once has a mink visited our camp, though we do see them at reasonably close range, hurrying across the meadow. On the evening of the mink's visit, we'd had a late supper after fishing until nearly nightfall. We had moved away from the table to sit by the fire with coffee before clearing away the scraps from our meal. Some slight movement caught our attention; we looked up and saw the most unexpected of visitors.

Sitting at the very edge of the table furthest from us was a mink, its late-summer fur glistening with long dark-brown cover hairs, its whiskers twitching in unison with the puckering and expanding of its small shining black button-nose. After the first involuntary turning of our heads we did not move but sat totally still, gazing at the animal. The mink stared at us in turn, appearing to be just as engrossed in observing humans as humans were in observing mink. Its examination was olfactory as well as visual; its nose kept up its constant twitching, trying to scent us or the food scraps on the table while its eyes were watching us.

That we did not move seemed to assure the mink that we'd do it no harm. It turned its attention to the food scraps. Apparently, mink enjoy trout, for it nibbled at the tails and fins and bits of flesh clinging to the bones on our plates. It sniffed at but did not touch the remains of bread and potatoes, nor did it pay any attention to the bowl of sliced cucumbers in a mildly vinegared sauce or the butter exposed on a saucer. It spent several minutes nosing a slice of lemon peel, but we could not see whether it flicked out its tongue to taste the lemon.

Its exploration of the table finished, the mink returned its full attention to us. It moved around the table until it was little more than a yard from where we sat, and in the light shed by our camp lantern we could see it very clearly. When it stopped and eased upright on its haunches the long black claws on its forepaws and the details of its elongated muzzle were quite distinct. From time to time it pulled its lips back from its teeth, which were sharp and shining white. From the small dot of a nose, its muzzle tapered to a rising rounded head, set on a long neck. Its body was round and elongated, its tail surprisingly thin and only half as long as its body and was very sparsely furred. Its hindlegs were hidden by its body, but our eyes were caught and held by its fur gleaming silkily in the yellow lantern light.

Somehow the mink's stance seemed to convey both relaxation and tension; though at ease, it appeared ready to move instantly. How quickly it could move was demonstrated graphically. Though it seemed much longer, the mutual survey we and the mink were making of one another lasted about ten minutes; then my wife or I made some slight inadvertent movement and the mink dissolved. We had been watching it closely, but when we compared notes later we agreed that neither of us had seen the animal move. One instant the mink was sitting on its hunkers on the edge of the table, the next it was gone; the word "dissolved" is not far-fetched. Never have we seen an animal vanish with such smoothness and speed—to end a moment of quiet wonder, one of many the high country has given us.

In the mountains as on the prairie, the coyote has gotten a

bad reputation; it suffers from what modern public relations practitioners call a "negative image." That was acquired by the plains coyote and transferred to its mountain cousin, which looks like the prairie breed and has many of the same habits. Prairie coyotes got the blame for herd depredations committed by the big prairie wolves. The wolves, of course, made no distinction between the herds of deer, antelope and buffalo they had hunted since the beginning of their history, and the cattle herds. Wolves are wanton killers, one of the very, very few animals that slaughters for sport as well as food. The plains coyote followed the wolves to scavenge, and got the blame for what the wolves had done. Because there were always more coyotes than wolves, the coyotes were more visible.

There were no trained naturalists around in the days of early settlement, and when naturalists did arrive a few score years later and tried to explain the coyote's scavenging habits and its preference for killing small animals like rabbits and prairie dogs rather than cattle and sheep, nobody was inclined to listen. The negative image had already been too well established, and when settlers began moving into the Sierra they brought with them the picture of the coyote as a herd-ravager. In effect, the coyote-haters said, "Don't confuse us with facts, our minds are made up." The bad and generally unjustified image attached to the prairie coyote was transferred to the mountain breed.

Unlike their flatland cousins, mountain coyotes do not hunt in packs. Mountain coyotes are loners. Even mated pairs do not always get along together, or stay mated any longer than is necessary to bring their pups to a precocious maturity. Once their family responsibilities have been discharged, mountain coyote pairs separate and remain apart until the mating season begins at summer's end. Then the animals do form small packs, seldom more than three or four pairs. It is only in late summer that we hear the packs yowling at night from the high ridges that overlook the lake.

Mountain coyotes are smaller than their prairie relatives, and are not even as big as a three-month fawn. They can neither overtake nor pull down a full-grown deer; any deer killed by a coyote is one that is sick and weak or injured, and we have seen tracks that showed where a doe had successfully defended her fawn from a prowling coyote. About the biggest animal the mountain coyote will attack is a marmot, and most of their hunting is confined to even smaller animals: gophers, moles, ground squirrels, mice. They eat the eggs and fledglings of ground-nesting birds, and vary their diets with tree buds, manzanita and currant berries, ripe flower-buds and insects. When no other food is available they eat grass and weeds to fill their complaining stomachs.

Coyotes do not come down to the lake, or at least none has done so while we were camped there. They prefer the ridges above it, thinly wooded timber-line areas where the soil is sparse over granite bedrock, and where burrowers cannot tunnel deeply. When the snowdrifts pile up at high altitudes, the coyotes drift downslope, but even before the snow melt begins they start returning to their favorite higher ranges. On perhaps a dozen late-summer nights the mournful song of the coyotes drifts down to our camp. They are distant, we know, because a coyote's midnight mourning heard any closer than three or four miles away sounds as though the singer is just inside the circle of light cast by one's campfire. Heard at any distance short of a half-mile, the coyote's call most closely resembles the noise of a nearby pre-diesel locomotive exhausting its steam with a final whistle-blast. It is perhaps the loudest sound a camper in the high country will hear.

Quite justifiably, coyotes distrust humans. Until the late 1960s, a bounty was paid for coyote tails, and only after the mountain coyote had almost been wiped out did the bounty payments stop. When we walk the high ridges we see their tracks and droppings, and the torn soil where they have hunted by night. Very rarely we will see one at dusk, retreating ahead of us, or heading for its rocky den. More than most animals, the coyote avoids humans; it is a trait acquired by any species that men have set out to kill.

THE DAY

TWELVE

Familiarity acquired through many years of visits has not lessened the pleasure of returning to the lake each summer. The Sierra high country has many faces, and while there is a strong family resemblance between them, no two are exactly alike, nor do any of them present exactly the same look from one year to the next. This is a quality of the land that prevents it from being grasped by an occasional visit, a passing observation. A summer in the high country is not like one at lower altitudes, where the season arrives after a leisured spring that has already revealed the sameness of the land, a sameness that winter did little to alter. In the mountains, summer's unfolding is swift, and reveals change superimposed on change; as it advances the land alters its appearance from day to day, even from hour to hour.

Many of the changes are subtle, revealed fleetingly as the summer climbs the slopes, winter quickly retreating before it. On the granite ridges that overlook the lake on one side and on the sloping sides of the forested valley that cuts between lake basin and peaks on the other side, the high country takes on different faces. Seen from the meadow below, the serrated horizontal lines of the ridges and the broken profile of the topmost ridge against the sky seem to retain the same contours, but as they are approached and seen close at hand, the changes appear.

A man-high boulder that served as a trail guide has split during the winter and fallen open in two almost equal halves that now lie low, invisible from below. Before the snow began, the brush on one of the shelves caught fire from a lightning-blast and the shelf, last year thickly-grown, is bare. A tree that clung to precarious life at the very rim of a line of exposed high granite fell to a winter gale; it lies, still green, on the loose scree below the ridge. None of these or other changes are visible when we set out to mount the huge steps up to the rim.

Starting from our camp beside the lake, at 7,500 feet, we walk just under three miles to the last ridge, 2,000 feet higher, the final step of a staircase hewed to a giant's scale. No real climbing is required, though in places the way up is steep enough to involve scrambling, and in other places a walker must lean sharply forward and make slow progress with short steps. From a distance the ridges present an illusion of sheer vertical cliffs rising in set-backs, one above the

A walk to the topmost ridge requires three full hours. There are tricky bare expanses covered with a loose, pebble-crusted soil. Each forward step must be taken with care.

other, but from their bases they can be seen to slant. Their formation is generally granitic, but it is broken here and there by basaltic intrusions, soft crumbly rock that erodes rapidly and deposits expanses of loose scree at the foot of the rise.

A walk to the topmost ridge requires three full hours. The three miles it covers when measured on a map in a straight line becomes more than double that distance in actuality. High country walking almost always requires detours from the straight line that in the level lowlands would be followed from point to point. Not only are a few truly vertical cliffs to be skirted and stretches of loose scree to be avoided, there are steep slopes that must be mounted in a zigzag path if they are to be traversed without going on hands and knees. There are tricky bare expanses covered with a loose coarse pebble-crusted soil that at best affords insecure footing; here each forward step must be taken with care, grinding a foot into the earth and scuffing out a small depression in which a boot sole can be securely cradled. To move otherwise is to risk a slide of fifty or sixty feet, and a hard stop at the bottom.

Where there is granite, occasional sheer stretches of vertical cliffs must be circled, and the treacherous honeycombed rocks that compose the scree must be avoided. Between each ridge the land is almost level, but it is not smooth. Bedrock lies near the surface here, covered by only a thin and friable skin of soil. Everywhere on the level shelves there are rock outcrops, solid boulders bigger than houses, jagged spears as tall as a man, rounded stones like bleached skulls, small fist-sized stones that shift underfoot.

Walking is easier across the shelves, however. Groves of trees stand on them, where chipmunks and chickarees stop their endless search for food to stare at the unaccustomed humans invading an area where people are seldom seen. Birds sit at arm's length without interrupting their twittering songs. A marmot that has left the meadow to summer on a shelf sits on the trunk of a long-dead tree and turns its head to peer solemnly, unwilling to interrupt its sunbath but alert to the presence of strangers.

In the tree clumps between and around rock outcrops on the shelves that push back from the crestline of each ridge to the base of the ridge above it, pines and firs intermingle. In this part of the Sierra high country there are no sharp cutoff lines marking the end of one kind of vegetation or animal or bird life and the beginning of another. The growth-zones occur at higher and at lower altitudes in sharp divisions, but this is the fortunate area where most types of plant and animal life merge and overlap.

Between the ridges, then, there are yellow pines and silvers, Jeffreys, lodgepoles and whitebarks; red and white and Douglas firs; a few scattered hemlocks, some isolated incense cedars, and, on the knolled crests, Sierra junipers. These do not grow in uniform numbers, of course. Pines and Douglas firs are most numerous, hemlocks and cedars appear only now and then at the edges of groves, sometimes standing aside from all other trees. Nor are the groves as thick as in the valleys, the shallow soil does not hold enough moisture or nutrients to support luxuriant stands.

In one way this is fortunate. Given the scanty number of trees and the difficulty and cost of pushing trails for haul-out trucks across the ridges, there is little likelihood that these stands will ever be lumbered. Here, nature will be left free to function without man's tinkering, as it has functioned for untold thousands of centuries. On these shelves between the ridges the primal Sierra will remain undisturbed.

Ascent of the ridges is rapid in terms of altitude. As each new ridge is topped the air grows thinner; lungs are a bit more difficult to fill to capacity. Stops to rest must be made more often. Feet in heavy hiking-boots gain weight and thigh muscles must be persuaded to exert the extra effort required to lift them. There are still ridges above when the effects of increased altitude are noticed. The crests are closer than they were an hour or two ago, but still look incredibly far off when the mind translates the distance measured by eyes into the number of steps that must be taken to reach them.

Finally the rise leading to the last crest is mounted, foot by plodding foot. The rocky summit is attained. Going up this ultimate slope the tops of trees on the shelf below have fallen away. Now there is nothing between you and the sky except the towering tips of the few pines that have managed to find root and grow in this unprotected spot. The tips of many of these trees are splintered, broken off in abrupt, rough, jagged ends, and their trunks are scarred by deep white gashes. These are the marks of lightning bolts, fire from the sky. This is where lightning strikes, at things that stand tallest in the highest places.

Ahead and behind as well as above there is only the sky. Beyond the crest stretches the tumbled granite, broken by green islands of trees and studded with the blue dots of distant lakes, and past its wide grey expanse are other ridges rising to peaks. Some of these are higher than the rim on which you stand, but they do not seem to tower over you; you stand at shoulder level with them, on equal terms. Looking back, the giant steps just ascended drop to the hand-sized patch of blue-green that is the lake. The ridges look less formidable from the crest. Soon you must go back down them, but there is time to rest a while, to thread along the broken rim with cautious steps. Exhaustion is forgotten, and the way back will not be hard. Except where scree is encountered, it is always easier to descend than it is to climb.

Walking the valleys on the side of the lake opposite the ridge requires less effort than the scramble up the great granite staircase, and brings an equal but different reward. There are no sheer cliffs rising in dramatic verticals that must be detoured, although in places the valley sides are too steep even going down to be navigated in a straight line. These more precipitous slopes must be walked at an angle, back and forth, but always heading in the direction you wish to take. In the half-century since loggers were last here, the duff has piled up thick under the close-set pines, and in steep places the duff can be as tricky to walk over as scree.

Years of falling pine needles and cones, twigs and branches, bark and dust form the duff. At its bottom the needles are moist, beginning to turn into humus. Toward the surface they grow progressively drier, and on top the latest to fall are fresh, flexible, slick. Mixed with and covered by the needles are the cores of pinecones that have been

A creek running through the meadow adds a grace note, the hurried purling of its passage over jagged stones between banks of fine gravel.

stripped of seeds, either by age or by chickarees; whole pine-cones; twigs as tiny as the lead inside a pencil and others as thick as a man's thumb; and branches of all sizes, some still holding bark, some bare. Most of the duff's components can be seen lying on its surface, but some are buried at its very bottom, having worked down to earth-level by their weight as the years passed.

There is a constant falling of small debris in a pine forest. Like everything in nature, the forests are in an endless cycle of death and rebirth. The cycle shows clearly in the trees themselves. Fresh buds, tomorrow's cones, form beside last year's cones; both hold the seeds of tomorrow's trees. Drooping white snags of branches that died when the tree grew so tall that its lower branches were shaded from the sun now hang lifeless on the trunk. When these dead limbs are small enough and low enough to be reached and pulled off for kindling, they are called "squaw wood." When they are massive and high on the tree in loosened sockets they are called "widow makers," and are feared by loggers. The limbs that have died hang on the trees for years, until insects chewing the wood from inside weaken their base sections, or until a storm dislodges them.

All things from above, large or small, that fall to earth under the pines contribute to the duff. Some, like the needles, make it feel springy underfoot, but this very softness can be deceptive. Those who walk the forest a great deal learn to feel with each step for the trap of crossed windfelled boughs and leaning dead branches that may snap underfoot. There are places, too, where the duff lies thinly over big smooth stones on which a boot sole will skid. Progress through a long-undisturbed pine forest is very like that made over steep slopes of shifting gravel, a matter of short steps taken with care.

There is no need to hurry. The forest will not move away, nor will the peaks around it. There is time to stop and sit down on a large stone or on the trunk of a deadfall and study a tree uprooted by some twisting wind that toppled it and tore its roots from the soil, bringing up clinging clots of earth and stones around which rootlets had twined, perhaps bringing up the roots of a nearby bush as well. There is time to examine, while sitting on a weathered length of pine trunk, the pocket fungi that sprout along the cracked dead surface of wood that long ago was stripped of bark by time or perhaps by a bear seeking the grubs of borers between bark and wood, and to trace with a fingertip the shallow rounded channels the borers cut in the trunk when it was still alive. There is time to stop beside the trunk of a massive yellow pine and find the source of a strange shining glint that

caught the eye, to discover that it comes from a drop of sap
oozing out of a woodpecker hole in the wound of an old
lightning-burn. The sap, crystallized, at a few moments each
day captures a slanting shaft of sunlight and glows like a
topaz.

Curving as they slope, or cutting in straight vees down the
flank of a mountain, the forested valleys open a succession of
vistas where the trees thin out. On some days the peaks seen
rising over the valley clefts seem unreachable, infinitely distant, but on days when the sky is filled with billowing high
swift-moving white clouds the far-off peaks are pushed
closer. When a summer rainstorm is building above the
peaks, the grey low-hanging clouds somehow diminish their
majestic heights. On other days, the air is neither clear nor
cloudy but is filled with a blue-white haze through which the
peaks and the forested valley floor over which they loom are
only vague shrouded ghosts. If the clouds are dark and thick
and low, the peaks are hidden and the pines foreboding and
lonely. Rain falling from high broken clouds isolated in expanses of sun-filled blue sky alternately obscures and reveals
the sloped valley walls and the peaks beyond. The vistas are
unchanged in their essence, but they are never quite the
same on two successive days.

Constant change also characterizes the high country's
sounds. Those who come to isolated places directly from
cities often remark on the quietness they find around them;
but unless they stay long enough for civilized noises to stop
ringing in their ears they will not become attuned to the
many voices of the mountains. Their ears are still filled with
the blatant stridencies that echo and re-echo through narrow
man-made canyons of concrete and steel and glass. Time is
required to allow ears thus assaulted to accept subtle sounds,
to realize that in the mountains there is no silence, but many
voices filling the thin clean air, and even the most isolated
places are never completely still.

Each small segment of the Sierra has its own voices, changing with the days and different in daylight from in darkness.
In the highest places the voices may be thin. Here, they
blend into a whispering of wind brushing across ragged

granite surfaces broken by clinging, leathery lichens, with perhaps a subdued solo from the branches of a solitary wind-warped pine or juniper. In the dense forest the voices are lustier, heavy with the rustle of branches, punctuated by the cries and movements of animals and birds. On meadows the voices are softer, yet more audible than whispers, a background of subtly-modulated tones of blowing grasses cut by the sharper notes of a rustling bush. Beside a lake the wavelets rippling against the shore are joined to the fugue. In every part of the high country the individual notes that make up a melody will differ in sound, pitch, intensity, duration, and often this change takes place within a distance of a few paces.

A breeze moving through a stand of close-limbed silver or whitebark pines whispers gently; the same volume of wind passing through the wide-spaced boughs of Jeffrey or limber lodgepole pines takes on a note of shrill urgency. The type of trees is not all that gives a forest's voice its character. Before entering the trees even a light wind that passes over brushfields—manzanita or willow, bitterbrush or deerweed—will cut the wind into distinctive notes. Or a sharp-angled cliff or valley may send the wind into the trees as whirling eddies, close to the ground or high in the air, so that no two groves of whitebarks or silvers or Jeffreys or lodgepoles or yellow pines speak with precisely the same voice.

A breeze in passing over a meadow may evoke only the soft sighing of squawgrass; it may rub together tall stalks of larkspur or lupine, or be thinned as it goes between the slender stems of lavender-buttoned pussypaws. In early summer a zephyr will be slit by the thick, wide leaves of skunk cabbage as it blows across a wet meadow; in late summer the same zephyr will change tone when it leaves the skunk cabbage patch. The leaves will then be brown and dry, and will impose a light staccato rattle on even the faintest-stirring air. A creek running through the meadow adds a grace note, the hurried purling of its rushing passage over jagged stones or the soft susurrus of imperceptible eddies as it slips between banks of fine gravel over a clean bottom.

Where the soil is rocky and strewn with uprooted trees, thin edges of narrow rocks caught in the rain-washed roots put a sharpness into the wind's voice and add a high note to the medley making up a meadow's sound. The shrill whistles of marmots, the almost inaudible squeaks of mice, the thin chittering of ground squirrels, all add their notes. In the pines these different tones will come from the chirking of chipmunks, the scolding of chickarees, the raucous calls of jays, the trebles and altos of bluebirds and juncos and sparrows, and the tapping tympanic rhythms of woodpeckers.

Different voices mark the day's periods: morning, noon, evening. Not all animals and birds are early risers. Some appear to have the same trouble humans do in awakening and forcing themselves to begin a new day. The small birds move first. They leave their nests, feathers still moist from the night's mist, and seek the highest branches of the tallest trees, where the sun will touch first. They perch, preening sleepily, fluffing their feathers and stretching their wings and tiny toothpick legs until the sun bathes and dries them. Only then do they fly off in search of seeds or insects for breakfast.

Soon after the nuthatches and juncos, chickadees, and warblers stir, the larger birds begin waking. The woodpeckers get busy, then the robins and bluebirds, and finally the jays. Later still, the hawks come out. After the birds, come the chickarees, and like the birds they first seek a branch at the tip of a soaring pine where they sit for perhaps a half-hour, scratching and grooming, before skittering down the bole to a laden branch to cut one of the cones for their day's first meal.

Next come the earth-nesters, chipmunks and ground squirrels. They wait until the dew-wet grass has dried in the sunshine before they begin to forage. Quite late in the morning the marmots emerge, and nibble at the succulent tips of meadow grasses between intervals of sunbathing. The small vegetarian meadow and forest creatures that feed by night have long hours past returned to their burrows, while in the grey moments between light and dark one of the feral animals can be glimpsed, making its way home. Deer usually start for their bedding-places shortly before the sky shows grey, but may choose to stay out until full day, especially in early summer when nights are short and the meadows green with lush fresh growth.

Unless a day is dark and cloudy, bird and animal activity slackens during the hour or so before the sun reaches its zenith, and a semi-halt can be felt in the land's pulse until the sun has begun its downward slide. During this period birds perch and animals nest to escape the harsh rays of light that come from directly overhead, penetrate the areas of forest

When the air is neither clear nor cloudy, it will be filled with a blue-white haze. Peaks and the forested valley floor are only vague shrouded ghosts.

that are usually shadowed, and destroy the sanctuary of dusky hiding places under bushes and at the roots of meadow grass. The little vegetarians feel more comfortable under a slanting light that provides shady areas for concealment and reveals the shadow of the circling hawk, chief enemy of the meadow-dwellers.

On days when there are intermittent clouds, which are almost always days of higher than usual winds, the birds stay near their nests, the small animals close to their dens or burrows. This does not indicate an aversion to being abroad in bad weather. It is rather a caution born of instinct. A lack of shadows on grey days, and a high wind that ruffles continuously the trees and grass and fills the air with rustlings—both mask the approach of predators from the air or on the ground. On sunny days when there is shade close by for concealment, when moving shadows are clearly defined, and when the wind is light and even and dies to periods of stillness, enemies signal their approach: the hawk casts a shadow, making its searching circles; the badger or weasel or marten disturbs the vegetation in either meadow or forest; and their intended prey have time to hide or flee.

Each high-country daytime cycle, then, speaks with a voice modulated in the fashion of a symphony: repeated themes developed with different instrumentation that always lets the melody come through, though with changed harmonies.

Above 6,000 feet in the Sierra most summer nights are almost windless. A day may have been briskly breezy, but it is an unusual night when the wind does not fade perceptibly shortly before sunset and die completely by the time it is fully dark. Around the shores of lakes, air convection creates the illusion that the wind is blowing lightly from the center of the lake to its edges, but even while this false breeze is felt near the shoreline the center surface of the lake is glass-smooth. The phenomenon is more readily noticed along the banks of large lakes than of small ones, but that is an illusion too.

Most of the noises of both forest and meadow subside as twilight deepens. Except for the owls, the birds perch early. The ground squirrels vanish even before the sun has set, and chipmunks seek their nests soon after twilight sets in. On the meadows the mice come out, and soon after that the hunters start arriving. Occasionally the stillness is broken by a rustle of grass or the scraping of claws in the soil. Willows along the creeks may clack softly as their branches are disturbed by a shoreline hunter—a mink or fisher—or by a deer pushing between them to drink from the stream.

Night or day, there is always more noise in the forest than on the meadows. Pinecones drop at all times; other sounds mask their fall during daylight hours, but in the relative stillness of the night the cones crash loudly from limb to limb and land with subdued thuds on the soft carpet of duff around the trees. In a stand of Jeffreys, the big heavy cones sound like sudden crackling thunder as they rattle off the limbs on their way down; the cones of yellow and silver pines are smaller, lighter, but almost as noisy in their falling. Even the squatty lodgepole cones and those from white-barks, loose and rounded, make surprisingly loud noises as they ricochet from one branch to the next.

Night noises are perhaps more impressive because their sources are mysterious, difficult to identify. Their point of origin is usually impossible to pinpoint, and darkness seems to have the power to multiply sounds. When there is light, a reasonably patient observer can almost always trace a sound to its source. Usually it will be found to be a chipmunk or bird or perhaps a pair of touching branches rubbed together when moved by the faint current of warm air rising from the sun-warmed earth. The listener is affected by knowing that night is the time when the hunters go abroad. A dead branch crackling spontaneously in the daytime is no reason for alarm, but when the same branch cracks at night there is the uninvited thought that it might have been stepped on by a prowling bear. It seldom is, but the thought is enough in itself.

At no hour during the night are the forest or the meadows totally silent, but in each twenty-four-hour cycle one time arrives when all the noises of both are subdued. For the brief period of transition from dark to daylight there is quiet. The nocturnals have gone back to their nests or dens, the daylight movers have not yet aroused. The breeze that comes with sunrise on most mornings has not begun to stir; the sun is still hidden by the eastern heights. Then and only then, and for a span of time so brief it must be measured in minutes, there is total stillness.

No bird calls trill, no brush or grasses stir, the tips of the tallest pines are motionless. In the east, dawnlight shows a leaden grey that rapidly brightens to a nacreous luster, the sheen of a perfect pearl. Within the space of a dozen heart-beats the sky shades from silken white to palest pink to the very faintest blue. Rays from the sun burst in shafts above the peaks, the blue in the sky deepens, the arc of the sun itself becomes visible. A fine smoke-mist begins to rise wherever water stands or flows and from the wet heads of the meadow grass. A single bird call breaks the hush. The day begins.

H UNTED

THIRTEEN

Only when the short summer season is almost at an end, its life a matter of days or even hours, is there anything that can be described as sustained human activity in the high country around the lake. This is the time when the Sierra deer-hunting season opens, and venison-hungry hunters go into places that are ignored or overlooked by others who visit the mountains between snows. The activity lasts only a few days, two weekends at most, much less if the weather is wet or cold or if an unusually early snow has brought winter prematurely. Oddly, fewer hunters come to the lake or pass by it than before the use of all-terrain vehicles became both a status symbol and an outlet for pent-up frustrations.

Once the lake was an easy walk of just a few minutes from the closest point of access by car, but a new road has been built about a mile from the old one, and few of today's hunters will walk that far from their machines. Since the entrance of the old logging trace that ended at a felled pine has been barred, we have hauled in our supplies with a one-wheeled rubber-tired cart, a sort of flatbed wheelbarrow. The new road runs between the meadow and the ridges, and along the half-mile that is nearest the lake there is only one flat spot where a car can be turned off, which we selfishly block with our own.

Today's motorized hunters do not like to go far from the security their vehicle represents to them. We hear them passing on Friday evenings, a gibbering of jeeps and a popping exhaust-whirr of bikes disturbing the quiet road with the nervous screech of motors accelerated beyond capacity, polluting the clean air with exhaust fumes before they leave, late Sunday. One reason we see fewer hunters today than formerly is the new habit that all-terrain vehicles have created. Hunters now tour superficially with the aid of wheels and noisy motors that frighten the deer instead of moving quietly on foot. A quick drive through the readily accessible areas is today's habit of the motor-borne hunters; if the ride brings no sight of game, they move on to another spot. Very rarely will motorized hunters return to an area they have driven across.

Our own venison will be hanging before noon of the first legal hunting day. This does not imply exceptional skill on my part. It reflects only familiarity with the terrain. Before the deer season arrives, I will have learned the deer trails within a reasonable distance from camp and on the first morning of the season will have gone out before daybreak to wait beside the most promising. One of my most valuable lessons in hunting I learned early, to find a deer trail and wait for the deer to come to me rather than yoicking over the slopes looking for them. The tactic is not as successful now as it was when hunters moved quietly, but so far it has brought a deer on the first day of each hunting season.

Several years have now passed since hunting and hunters began to be abused. The chief abusers are metropolitan sufferers from the Bambi syndrome who have never set foot off pavement, or those emotionally aroused as a result of malicious misinformation, or those who think opposition to hunting politically expedient. I've often been asked why I continue to hunt. Frequently the question comes from young friends who know my general attitude of *laissez-faire* toward animals, but who themselves have been taught that for some unstated reason, humans are required to protect all animals equally. None of them have hunted, few have any first-hand knowledge of mountain ecology, but they are honestly and seriously concerned, and they deserve honest, serious answers.

This is my reply. There is no single simple reason that keeps me hunting. A number of personal and impersonal factors are involved. My first reason is purely selfish: I like the flavor of well-cooked venison, though I would forego the enjoyment if deer were an endangered species. They are not. My second reason is that with a general decline in hunting skills, in most areas the deer population is greater than the land can support; hunting replaces natural herd-limiting factors that no longer operate. Finally, over the years I have seen several hundred carcasses of deer that died of old age or winter starvation. It would have been better had most of these died from a hunter's bullet, which kills cleanly and quickly, rather than starve. And the meat from these starved deer would then have been used, not wasted.

In the wild, a deer has a maximum life expectancy of six to eight years. By its sixth year its teeth wear smooth and begin to break up. A few strong animals escape this, but by their eighth year at most a deer cannot browse on the rough wild growth to which it turns in winter when soft graze is not available. If the deer lives in a place where soft grazing is found the year around, its life expectancy is lengthened by a year, perhaps by two or three. Even if it lives this long, it will not be in prime condition or good health. If it is a buck, its reproductive function has been usurped by younger, more vigorous animals; if a doe, it has become barren. As a deer's teeth deteriorate, so does its entire physical tone. In hard-grazing areas such as the high country, a deer grows progressively weaker, unable to eat during snow months, and dies from starvation or disease.

Some opponents of any kind of hunting are anthropomorphists, who attribute human traits to animals. They forget that deer, like all animals, differ in mentality from humans. As far as can be discovered, only the human mind has the ability to live in the tomorrow, to look forward and plan for a distant future. Animals know only the today, the now. More emotional and less well-informed antihunters equate hunting with blood lust, the thrill of killing. This is balderdash. Few hunters live in anticipation of the final shot alone, or experience a perverse *frisson* at the sight of blood or death. What is most rewarding to a majority of those who hunt is the period before finger seeks trigger, the pitting of brain and skill against the strongest of all instincts, survival. Hunting deer is actually a contest of amateur against professional, because to live to its prime any wild animal must become a professional in the art of surviving. It is the human hunter who is the amateur, operating in the deer's terrain, and the far-reaching bullet does not equalize the odds. Most honest hunters will admit that luck as much as skill accounts for whatever success they have.

We enjoy eating venison and utilize every scrap of it we get, but this does not detract from our pleasure in watching deer just for the sake of watching them. There is no overt purpose in our minds when we watch; we do not mentally translate each deer we see into bundles of chops and steaks and roasts.

All around the lake there are deer trails and beside them spots where we can sit quietly and watch bucks and does and fawns move past, some only a few yards away. For four years in succession we watched one doe, and are sure it was the same doe each year, for she was of a distinctive shade of red we have seen on no other Sierra deer. Summer after summer for those four years we saw her several times each season, coming to drink at the lake late in the evening, or on the trails, or grazing in the meadow. There was always a fawn at her side. Then, one year we did not see her, and we have seen her no more.

One of the challenging pastimes offered by the high country is a bloodless test of skill against instinct that matches human against deer. It is possible, though many people doubt it, to walk up within arm's length of a deer under certain conditions and by observing two simple precautions. The conditions are that the deer be grazing with head down, its attention focused on feeding, and that the wind be blowing away from them; besides, the individual making the approach must have reasonable physical control and extreme patience. The precautions are that no white garment be worn, or any clothing with widely contrasting colors, and that observation of the deer never slacken.

Given those conditions and precautions, it is really not too difficult to walk very close to a deer in the wild. The approach must be slow, one small half-step at a time. Each foot, before it is set down, must explore the ground under it to avoid a dry branch or loose rock that would cause a sharp, sudden noise. An approach of this kind may require half to three-quarters of an hour to complete, and during that time, observation of the deer must never let up. Grazing deer habitually signal their intention to raise their heads by twitching their muscles in the neck-shoulder area and by erecting and holding still their ears, which have been twitching constantly. This is the clue to stop any motion, even if a foot is raised in mid-stride it must be halted and held immobile until the deer resumes grazing.

Often when grazing deer look up, they turn their heads to sweep the landscape with their eyes, though they depend much more heavily on the senses of smell and hearing than vision. But, while they do not see colors vividly, deer are very sensitive to white, which is a shade alien to nature, and to extreme color contrasts. However, if the approach is made at the rate of eight to ten inches with each step, noiselessly, and by freezing when the animal raises its head, a person can get close enough to touch a deer.

Actually, it is not a good idea to get that close. From a distance of a yard or a bit more a deer can scent a human even if a strong wind is blowing from the deer toward the person. When it gets the human scent, the deer is likely to panic, and panicky deer are unpredictable at such close quarters. The deer may run, or it may choose to defend itself. Deer attacking a human do not gore with their antlers, as cattle do with their horns. Both bucks and does attack with their forefeet, the front edges of which are razor-sharp. They can inflict dangerous wounds.

Walking to within a few feet of a deer is a challenge, a test of outdoor skill. Even if the approach aborts and the deer runs while still fifteen or twenty feet away, the stalker can consider the approach a victory. Nor is it always wasted: unless its panic is extreme, a bolting deer usually runs only a short distance before stopping in cover to listen and smell, and if nose and ears bring no messages of alarm, the deer will generally go back to grazing. Since a deer in panic blunders through the brush with about as much stealth and quiet as a clumsy cow, its location can in most cases be spotted.

If the grazing area from which it bolted is unusually rich, it may well return in a quarter-hour or so. The strategy for the

human is to sit down quietly in an unobtrusive spot, prefera-
bly in the shade where he can blend with a tree trunk or
stump, a boulder, or a brush pile. Then, if his patience
matches that of the deer, he can try the walking-up stunt
again.

Sitting or standing silently is always a profitable tactic
when starting out to watch wild animals of any kind. Most of
them depend on their senses in the reverse order from
humans; while we rely first on our eyes, then our ears, and
finally our noses, the animals do not. For distant clues to the
approach of enemies they smell the wind, then listen while
standing immobile, and finally confirm with their eyes what
nose and ears have told them. In the high country, where
winds often eddy unpredictably, it seems to me that many
animals have come to rely less on scent than on hearing.
Even if conditions are not ideal for a downwind approach,
one should be tried in the event a wind eddy between you
and the animal might carry your scent away.

Animals are never totally predictable; their instincts are
often modified by conditions or circumstances, and there are
no hard-and-fast rules that cover the behavior of any species
at a given moment. Cougars, for example, have perhaps the
keenest combination of senses—eyesight, scent and hearing—of all large feral beasts. They are also more than
ordinarily wary of men, having been the target of bounty
hunters for more than a century. Only at the end of the
1960s, after the Sierra Nevada cougar population had been
reduced to perhaps as few as 500 in the entire range did
California abolish the fifty dollar bounty it had been paying
since the 1850s for dead cougars, and give the animals at
least that token protection.

As rare as they are, cougars are still seen occasionally, and
as wary as they are it is still possible to approach them fairly
closely under ideal conditions. In their case, this would mean
a hungry cat eating a late breakfast after a long night's hunt.
There are, incidentally, no known instances of a cougar's attacking a human being. But they do take deer, usually the
old and crippled ones that are too weak to escape the big
cat's leap. Very probably cougars also kill a few fawns each

year, though given the migrating pattern of the main Sierra deer herds, fawns are usually able to escape a cougar by the time the herds return to the high altitudes the cats favor.

Bobcats, the small stub-tailed relatives of the cougars, live at lower altitudes than their big cousins. In spite of their small size—bobcats seldom weigh over 20 pounds—they are aggressive hunters and probably account for many more fawn deaths in a year than do cougars. These little members of the lynx clan prey chiefly on the small meadow-animals, though. They hunt ground squirrels, chipmunks, gophers, mice, and consider ground-nesting birds and their eggs a real delicacy. Though bobcats avoid men with a fervor equal to that of the big cats, they are not as wary of human habitations, such as campsites; we see bobcat tracks regularly, the cats themselves very, very rarely.

Black bears, the only other large surviving predators native to the Sierra, are neither as shy nor as rare as the cats. Bears range far more widely in terms of altitude as well as in relation to their home dens, if indeed they have a single fa- vored den. Cougars and bobcats rarely stray more than three or four miles from their rocky dens hidden in the high granite; bears have no summer dens and are extremely mobile. A mature bear in the high country may travel twenty miles within twenty-four hours.

Bears hibernate at altitudes above 7,500 feet, but drop downslope in early summer and range between snow line and timber line until the time comes for them to hibernate; then they go back to the heights. Since men wiped out the California grizzly a half-century ago—the last surviving specimen was seen in 1924—and since the big timber wolves were exterminated even earlier, there have been no animals in the high country that will attack humans without provoca- tion. Even when it is anxious to begin its winter doze and un- happy from lack of sleep, even when it emerges from its den late in January or early in February as hungry as its name proverbially implies, the black bear will retreat instead of at- tacking.

Exceptions should be noted here. What we humans might

not consider provocation may be provoking to a bear. A female with cubs considers any nearby human dangerous to her young. In and around the national parks there are bears that have acquired the bad habits of Rocky Mountain grizzlies in the parks of those mountains, after being fed consistently by humans they are provoked when people do not offer them food. In both areas, by exposure to park visitors the bears have lost their fear of men, and thus have become dangerous.

New visitors to the Sierra are inclined to be nervous when bears are mentioned. Fresh in their minds are the highly publicized instance in the early 1970s when grizzly bears in the Rockies mauled and killed people in their sleeping bags and stories of bears ripping cars apart to get to food stored in them. These things did happen, of course, but the bears involved were grizzlies. Grizzly bears and black bears are as different in habits and reactions as South Sea Islanders are from Eskimos.

High-country bears have one bad habit, from the human standpoint. They consider themselves entitled to any food in the range they claim, which may be forty to fifty miles in diameter, and they do not distinguish between food brought in by campers and food that is provided by nature. When campers with sloppy habits leave highly scented meats such as ham and bacon or sweet things such as candy or cake in paper sacks or opened tins, they are inviting a bear in to dine. Once started, the bear will not be satisfied with the foods in bags or open cans; it will tear into every container it finds. A bear's strength is unimaginably great. Containers that it cannot open with its claws will be chewed apart. We keep a neat camp not merely because we like to be tidy, but because a clean camp will seldom be bothered by a passing bruin. So far, we have escaped.

Bears invading camps, drawn by the smell of food—and to a bear, human garbage is food—usually do so at night, and the startled camper's first reaction is to drive the animal away. The bear, equally startled, reacts to protect its food and itself; people and bears both tend to be a bit nervous when they come into close or unexpected contact. The bear may not be intending to kill, only to brush aside a human interfering with its meal. Being brushed aside by a bear is the rough equivalent of being run into by a bulldozer with claws.

We have seen more than one example of the tremendous power that is packed into the short, heavily muscled legs of a black bear. We have come across stumps torn apart to get at termites and ants inside them, and have seen huge tree-trunks flipped over like matchsticks by a bear searching for the grubs beneath their bark. We have seen more than the mute evidence, we have seen it happen.

In very early summer, returning from a dawn hike, we stopped beside a flooded meadow to decide which way it could best be crossed. The meadow was about three miles from the lake, and the last time we had visited it, it had not held a snow pond. Now, we had a choice of taking a long detour around it, or jumping from one to the other of the numerous rock outcrops that rose above the snow pond's surface. While we were trying to decide whether to hike the extra distance or risk falling in the knee-deep water if we misjudged a leap, a movement in the trees at the far side of the meadow caught our attention. It was less a movement than a changing pattern of light and shadow. We were sure we saw something, but not certain what we had seen.

We stood motionless. The shadow took on shape and definition, and we were looking at a large black bear. On the boggy ground between trees and meadow the bear stopped, raised its broad head and swung it from side to side, sampling the wind. Bears have notoriously bad vision. When testing their surroundings, they depend first on their sensitive noses, then on their sense of hearing. The wind was blowing our scent away from the bear, though we could not be sure that an eddy around the meadow might not exist. We heard the bear's sighing grunt when it was satisfied that the meadow was safe, and were surprised to see a cub emerge from the pine grove and come to stand beside its mother.

We were also more than a little concerned. Mother bears with young cubs along have short-fused tempers. We stood at the side of a high rock outcrop, some distance from any trees. By signs, we agreed to edge around behind the rocks at the risk of being seen by the bear. We made it without attracting the attention of the mother, and crawled up on the high chunks of granite to watch the two bears.

Food was obviously on their minds. A small cluster of tiger lilies was sprouting close to where they stood. The mother led the way to them, and in five minutes she and the cub had wiped out the lily patch. They ate hungrily, clawing the bulbs out of the mucky soil and eating them in gulps, ignoring the mud that clung to the bulbs. Now, the mother bear began to look for something more. She found it, a fresh windfelled pine—fresh meaning it had been down for only a year or two, not long enough for the bark to have fallen away.

After a few preliminary snuffs along the tree trunk, the old bear began tearing off the bark with quick swipes of her four-inch claws, uncovering the grubs and beetles that lay beneath it. Mother and cub thrust their muzzles into the bark that had fallen on the ground and with their tongues scooped up the insects that had fallen with it. They nuzzled into the chunks of bark for several minutes before turning their attention to the bared wood of the windfall, then they nosed along it, tongues lapping out to snare a larva or borer. The soft orange hue of rotting pine showed in several places along the trunk, a clue that the tree had been badly hurt, was indeed beginning to die, before it had toppled. The mother bear paid special attention to these spots, shredding away the decayed wood to expose more grubs and lapping them up with pleased grunts.

For something like thirty minutes the two bears worked over the exposed top and sides of the windfall, stripping away any of the bark that remained on it. After the big bole had been completely stripped of bark and insects the mother bear was still not satisfied. She began shoving at the tree-trunk, hindpaws braced in the yielding soil, forepaws digging and clawing along its bottom. When the cub tried to help her, she stopped pushing at the trunk long enough to shove the youngster aside. Then, bracing herself again, she arched her back and heaved. The tree trunk moved a few inches.

She dug her forepaws into it, near the ground, and with a quick lifting heave, turned the trunk over to expose the side that had been on the bottom.

At its root end the dead pine trunk was nearly three feet in diameter, and the section that she moved in one piece was about fifteen feet long. It was a load that would have challenged the strength of three sturdy lumberjacks working with peaveys to give them leverage, but the bear moved it unaided, in a demonstration of the unbelievable strength that was contained in her leg and back muscles.

Not until every inch of the newly exposed bark had been ripped away and exposed for insects did the bears stop feeding. It would be heartening to report that the mother bear fed her cub choice tidbits or gave it instructions on how to find food. This did not happen. The mother was quite obviously interested only in filling her own stomach. She offered not a morsel to the cub, nor showed it where to find one, and when the young bear got in her way, she shoved it aside roughly. The cub got only as much food as it could salvage unaided.

Certainly the cub was learning by example, and it's possible that we expected too much from the mother in the way of instruction and solicitude for seeing that the cub fed well. For all we know, the mother bear may have been instructing the young one in the growls and grunts she uttered from time to time, or communicating with it silently in the way animals often appear to do.

Our long period of watching at close range did give us a chance to observe the appearance and actions of the bears in detail. The mother was still gaunt from winter's hibernation, her belly sagged and her flanks were concave. She was just beginning to lose her frowsty cave-coat. Bears we have seen late in the summer in the high country had fur of a rich deep brown that in some lights looked black; this mother's coat was patched with light dead-looking fur. The effect was that of a very bad henna job on an aging woman's hair. The cub's fur was glossy, though, a medium-dark brown with a lighter area around its shining black muzzle. When on all-fours, the mother bear stood between three and four feet high at her shoulders, and her body was perhaps six feet long from muzzle to tail. The cub was not newborn, but a yearling, and was probably spending its last few months under its mother's supervision before being launched into the world to make its own way.

After their meal of grubs the two bears started around the snow pond. If they continued around it they would very soon reach the rock formation where we were hiding. We did not know whether to stay or retreat, and were beginning to get nervous when the mother bear spared us the need for making a decision. She waded out into the pond, the cub following her. For what seemed to us to be a very long time the two bears rolled and wallowed in the shallow water, scraping the bottom alternately with their bellies, sides and backs, occasionally standing semi-erect to shake in the habit of furred animals ridding themselves of water.

By this time we were getting both tired and hungry. We'd left camp early, while the dawnlight was just bright enough for us to see the path we'd followed on our hike. We'd planned to return in the early morning sunlight and eat, so had carried neither food nor water with us. It was now almost noon by the sun, and we saw no chance of getting off the granite formation as long as the bears were so close. We reasoned that if the mother bear could hear our voices but could not see us, she would not be able to attack us. Flattening as much as possible on top of the rocks, we started to talk loudly, raising our voices now and then almost to a shout. We could still hear the bears splashing in the water, and risked raising our heads to look.

Both mother and cub were wading out of the snow pond. On its bank, the cub headed for the trees, the mother stood looking across the water in our direction, trying to locate us from the sound of our voices. We could not tell whether or not she saw us, but we took the chance that she did not, and kept talking loudly. The wind had not changed direction, still blowing from the bears toward us. The big bear held her position for several minutes, swinging her head and shoulders from side to side, her broad head raised, her nostrils expanding and contracting. At last she decided to go. She loosed a disgusted "Whuff" and followed the cub into the trees.

She did not run; it was not a panicky retreat. She moved with haste, but deliberate haste, as if there were no good reason for a solitude-loving bear to risk staying where human voices could be heard. After the mother bear had vanished among the pines, we waited long enough to give the pair time to get well away from the area. Then we climbed down, skirted the snow pond, and went back to camp.

Several times while walking through thick stands of trees we have had distant encounters with bears, but the bears have always heard or scented us long before we were aware of their presence. We've heard them crashing through the brush in retreat, and on a few occasions have glimpsed them as they were loping away, but the only opportunity we have had for close observation was the time at the snow pond.

There was one year when an unusually early snowfall surprised us by arriving without the advance weather signals that almost always precede a snow. The fall was heavy but had stopped before daylight, and the day had dawned brightly with a warm sun. We were reasonably sure the snowstorm was a freak, for year after year we'd stayed much later than the time this snow arrived. Deer season opened on the morning after the snow, and I decided to go on with the hunt I'd planned. Usually such a premature snow will spook the deer and start them moving out of the high country, so my chance of having a buck come along the trail I'd planned to watch were reasonably good.

Leaving camp early, I went to the selected vantage point and waited, but no deer were moving; they'd apparently started their exodus downslope during the night. In mid-morning, I gave up and headed back to camp, taking a different trail in the hope of picking up a fresh track. There were tracks aplenty in the fresh snow. At one spot there was a trampled area a hundred yards wide where a deer herd had passed, heading for the grassy foothill valleys. It was impossible to count the number of deer in the herd, the surface was such a maze of overlapped hoofprints, half-filled with the snow that had fallen since the herd's passing. The tracks led over the hump of a ridge down into a valley, through which the herd would travel to the next valley, and so on downslope to the deer's winter range.

Deer tracks were not the only signs of animal movements the fresh snow held; there were the shallow prints of small animals as well. I detoured more widely than would have been the case had my interest not been held by the messages the virgin covering conveyed, and camp was still more than a mile away when the first bear tracks appeared on the softening snow.

Normally, I'd have examined the tracks, perhaps followed them a short distance, and then gone on my way, leaving the bear to go wherever it was heading. One of the pawprints, though, was bloodstained. At once I thought that the bear might have been wounded by a deer hunter, though I'd heard no shots during the entire morning. Then other possibilities came to mind. The animal might have been hit by a late-arriving hunter's car, or been creased with a pistol bullet when it raided a camp during the night.

A wounded, hurting bear is a clear and present danger to any human it encounters. In the mind of a bear, a wound is provocation that entitles it to attack any member of the species that inflicted the wound. I set out to follow the tracks, with the half-formed idea that if the wound was serious the bear should be killed before it came across a hunter or a deer camp and perhaps mauled someone.

Tracking was easy in spite of the warm sunshine that was rapidly softening the light powdery snow. Catching up with the bear was another matter. There was no way to time its passage at the point where I ran across its trail, but from the compact form of the bloodstains, which had not yet seeped deeply into the snow, it could not have been too long since the tracks were made. I followed the trail through the entire morning, with a growing feeling that I was steadily losing ground. When the bear came to some obstacle, such as a big pile of jackstrawed windfelled pines or a sheer rise of rock or a stream, it kept moving in a straight line regardless of what lay across the path it had decided to take.

There was no way that I could follow the trail over most of the obstacles; it was necessary to circle them and pick up the prints on their other side. For about two miles the tracks were deep and easy to follow. Then, the bear must have sighted me or scented me, for it began circling back on its trail in loops, and the spacing of its prints told me it was moving faster. Once or twice the prints described a figure eight through forested areas where the snow covered the ground only lightly. In these places, I had to circle the stand of trees to find the spot where the bear had emerged.

By noon I was exhausted and still had not gotten sight of the bear. My rifle was heavy in its sling, and my stomach was growling with hunger. I did not feel the same urgency to keep on the trail that I'd felt in the beginning. The bloodstains had grown steadily smaller, a sign that the animal's wound was quite probably superficial and was closing up. There was certainly no indication that its vitality was diminishing. Mine was. In midafternoon, when the tracks ended abruptly at an impossibly vertical granite face that the bear had apparently scaled, I gave up and returned to camp.

Looking back, I recall feeling relieved when the trail sign showed that the bear was not badly hurt. If I had caught up with it soon after crossing its tracks, with the thought uppermost in my mind of the possible danger a wounded bear represented, I would probably have killed the animal needlessly. Hunting game for meat gives me satisfaction, but useless killing does not. Playing the part of an executioner, even in a justified killing, does not appeal to me. And, by the time I'd reached the place where the trail ended, after the bear had so easily surmounted obstacles that defeated me, I had acquired a great deal of respect for its strength, stamina, and its instinct to survive.

Black bears are not yet among the Sierra's endangered species, as are cougars, wolverines, fishers, bobcats, ringtails and eagles. The black bear may never join this list, for if pressed too hard it can follow the example of the cougar, retreat to the highest, most barren ridges above timber line, and somehow, as has the cougar, manage to survive.

SUMMER'S END

FOURTEEN

For something over a quarter of a century now, we have watched the lake and have seen it and its basin and the high country around it in every aspect they can assume. Though our recognition has sometimes been belated, we have seen and noted the changes made by natural forces in the lake itself, the pine forest, the meadows, and the granite ridges. None of the alterations have been sudden or dramatic. They have almost universally been infinitesimal, so subtle that often we did not notice them as they were taking place, but only after the process of change was well advanced.

Rains and melting snow have washed earth from above the banks down into the water's margin, and in places the lake's shore line has extended minutely into the water. The extension of the land has not been large at any one spot, a few inches at best, and in most places not more than an inch or so. The most noticeable difference can be seen around the inflows, where the springs and creek have carried particles of vegetable debris and grains of sand or soil into the water and deposited them on the bottom. Along the inlets, the lake is now much shallower than it was when we first saw it.

Fewer areas around the shore line have stayed static than have changed; the ratio of alteration to stasis is roughly fifty or sixty to one. This may be because the changes elsewhere have been too gradual for us to notice. But the lake has grown shallower; it is almost imperceptibly losing surface area as well as depth. Decade by decade it is shrinking, and it cannot recover the areas it loses. This encroachment of land on quiet waters is as universal and inexorable as the erosion of soil by rivers and creeks and blowing winds. The process is slow, but it is irreversible. When enough centuries have passed, the waterborne and wind-blown grains of soil will absorb the lake. Its basin will be converted into a grassy meadow through which will wind two or three spring-fed creeks.

Change has not been confined to the lake. The flanks of the big granite bluffs overhanging its waters along part of the shore were seamed and cracked when we first saw them. Now, many of these cracks have widened and deepened and in some places slabs of the granite have been pushed off the bluffs' faces by the water that seeps into them and expands as it freezes. A number of what were once small cracks have become fissures wide enough to hold soil in which pussypaws and junipers and grasses and manzanita have rooted. Their roots push down into the depths of the cracks, where they are still hairline-thin, and rive the tough stone apart. In two or three spots this process has reached the point where chunks of granite as large as a small house or an automobile have fallen away from the mother rock.

Some of the separated pieces have fallen into the lake. Others are beginning to be broken into still smaller pieces by the action of water and wind and by the roots of plants. Eventually these huge boulders will become small stones, the stones pebbles, the pebbles grains. The same forces of wind and water will work on the plants that aided in reducing the rock. Their foliage will bloom and die, and when dead it will decay, adding humus to the grains of granite; in a few eons a fertile soil will be formed where once there were great expanses of granite.

Narrow margins of soil have already formed in a few places where the granite bluffs once dropped vertically into the lake. Pine seeds lodging on these strips have produced saplings that are growing into trees. Willows, once found only in isolated clumps along the creek and around the springs but rarely at the lake's rim, are now growing in a number of places on the shore line. Where broad expanses of the shallow water showed clear golden sandy bottom, loam has silted in to cover much of the sand. The loam has nutrients, as the sand did not, to support water plants that have spread into the shallows from the inlets.

Because they now have smaller stretches of current-washed shallows above sandy bottom on which to drop their eggs, the trout are diminishing in number. They are still plentiful, but they grow smaller in average size each

year. Between the spring that is our food-cooler and the spot
where we stretch our tarpaulin, the willows have crept inch
by inch. There is still more than enough area for our needs,
but going from our shelter to either the spring or creek has
become a matter of pushing through brushy willow-growth
instead of taking a few quick steps across bare ground.

More pines now grow in the forest that extends over the
lake basin to the rim of the deep valley beyond it. In places
where thick clusters of seedlings had sprouted there remain
only those that were sturdy enough to grow into saplings;
shaded by the healthier growth, the other saplings died.
Where saplings once grew, mature trees now stand. Here,
too, the sturdy crowded out the weak; the saplings that were
strong and healthy enough to resist the attacks of borers, and
those that did not break under the weight of deep snows
were those that matured.

A number of the big, old trees have rotted from their
hearts and toppled to earth. The biggest tree in the basin, an
isolated silver pine at the edge of the meadow beyond the
lake, was weakened by heart rot and fell in a winter storm. It
will one day bleach to a whitened skeleton, like those of
other earlier giants that died and fell. But the meadow itself
has changed only a little, and the smallest apparent change of
all has taken place on the granite ridges that rise like steps
past the meadow.

These changes are not death, but life. Within several centuries, ten, fifteen, the lake will very probably die, but in dying it will give birth to a meadow. When, after more
centuries, the pines creep out over it, the meadow will have
given birth to a forest. Men take two views of nature's ways.
One is the "Mother Nature" attitude, which praises all
natural workings as benign, kindly, friendly, and beneficial.
The other viewpoint, which its holders claim to be more
realistic, is that nature is stern, harsh, and cruel in its workings, and should be controlled by mankind. Neither viewpoint is correct. Nature is neither kind nor cruel—or is both,
and often at the same time. More to the point, nature simply
is.

Human understanding of nature's intricate ultimate forces

is scanty at best. Dimly we are gaining an insight into some of the basic rules or principles by which all living things are governed; in the past we have not bothered to learn the rules and as a result have lost a number of innings of the game, but not the game itself—not yet.

We—the human race—have long been conscious of "the Laws of Nature," and the endowment of men with "certain inalienable rights," but in our present days it is slowly seeping into our awareness that all natural things, sentient or insensate, are similarly endowed. We are even coming to understand that the endowment is not a free gift and that it is not perpetual. It is dawning on us that the gifts must be earned and will endure only as long as we do not violate too greatly the natural balances which are part of the endowment of the whole.

In the Sierra high country the struggle to earn and maintain the balances can be seen readily if we take the time and make the effort to look. Because the soil over most of the high country is thin, nearly all the plants and trees put down deep roots which are thickly matted, which prevents the summer winds from drying up too much of the scarce moisture. The tendrils on the roots reach into the deepest crevices; if they fail to do this, the plant dies before its seeds mature. Pines, thickly seeded in the duff, must send down a taproot to get a continuing supply of moisture. If the taproot strikes granite bedrock before reaching a water supply, the seedling will die. As trees mature, the healthy ones grow fastest and shade the slow growers; deprived of sunshine, the weaker seedlings die.

While browsing on the high country's sparse vegetation, deer must move almost constantly when the first lush greenery of summer has faded to brown. Their constant movement tones and keeps supple the muscles they need to make the sudden spring that will save them from the rush of animal predator or the bullet of a human hunter; in such times of danger, a spurt of speed is all that stands between the deer and death. Small areas of thick pasturage make deer lazy. They stay in one place, their muscles soften, and they fall to the leap of the cougar or fail to move fast enough to

escape the hunter's bullet. Bear and cougar vie for the right
to take weakened deer, and one falls before the strength and
agility of the other.

Baby chipmunks, ground squirrels, chickarees chase one
another in what humans call play, but it is play with a purpose. It sharpens the reflexes the small creatures need, and
keeps supple the muscles they call on to escape weasel or
bobcat or coyote. Mink and marten kits chase one another,
too, wheeling and darting from tree to tree, and this is also
called play by humans; but it serves the kits as does the
similar play of the smaller creatures that are their food. Bear
cubs wrestle and cuff each other, and this develops the
stamina and strength they will need in maturity; so does the
rough driving of the mother bear when she forces her cubs
to walk long miles each day, to dig, to strain. Bears have big
stomachs that always seem to be empty, and they must
forage over a wide area to keep themselves fed.

Only the mountains seem static, unable to move and
develop survival strengths, but theirs is the sum of all the
smaller strengths that touch them: plants, animals, sun, wind,
water. Roots and water combine to make the coarse soil fit
for growth. Animals and birds sow seeds in their droppings
and at the same time enrich the soil on which the droppings
fall. Washing waters create lakes, small lakes are transformed
into meadows. Trees encroach on the meadows and grow to
become forests. Lightning strikes the trees, fire destroys a
grove and loosens the soil. Manzanita and juniper hold the
loose earth in place and live on it until the seedlings these
brushes have sheltered grow to towering trees. These with-
hold light from the bushes, and they die. Water and wind
carry away the soil from a burned-over meadow; a basin
forms and becomes a snow pond, the snow pond a lake that
fills to become a meadow, which becomes a forest. The cycle
is inextricably interwoven and continues eternally unless
broken by forces outside nature. Man is the only creature
that has the ability to interrupt this cycle.

When we began to interpret the almost microscopic
changes we had noticed as signs that the lake would ultimately vanish, our feeling was one of loss. It was a

transitory emotion, however. Very little thought was needed to recognize and to accept the change as a natural cycle, universal, not confined to one small Sierra lake-basin. We came to understand that the change would take decades, perhaps centuries, to complete, and until it is far advanced the lake will remain much as it is, to delight us and others who have come to find pleasure in the many gifts such quiet places offer.

One thing that will remain unchanged for at least part of the lake's remaining life is its isolation. A ten-square-mile area at the edge of its basin has been designated as a wilderness area. It is closed to all wheeled vehicles, hunting within it is illegal, and it will not be logged again. The single rutted trace of a road that rambles through part of it will not be improved; no other will be built. This was why the new road was built several years ago; it replaced—rather, made inaccessible—the logging trace that we followed to within a short distance of the lake. We gladly trade the inconvenience of carrying our supplies in for the greater distance; the change means that the lake and its basin will be allowed to age naturally.

Earlier, I mentioned that the new road removes our camp even further than before from the spitting of motorbikes and the angry yowls of all-terrain vehicles. We see evidence of the spoilers elsewhere: crumpled beer and soda cans, broken bottles, charred remains of fires not extinguished safely with a layer of dirt, wads of metal foil and blobs of shiny plastic. Once we wondered why those who leave unsightly litter care so little about the unspoiled areas they have taken such pains to reach. Our saddening conclusion is that they are interested in reaching isolated spots only to be able to boast of the machines—which they had no part in creating—that made their visits possible.

One new dimension has intruded on the lake's solitude. When we first began camping there, aircraft flew low, only a short distance above the passes that they followed across the mountains. There were few planes then, but now jets pass over the lake two or three times a week, five miles above the peaks. The short angry cry they emit during their brief swift

passage reaches us a few moments after the jets have
vanished, as their white vapor trails slowly dissolve in the
sky.

At summer's peak the jet trails are as often as not the only
kind of clouds to be seen. Before summer reaches its midpoint there are genuine clouds nearly every day, white, high,
billowing, driven fast by shifting winds. For a few weeks then
the sky is completely clear before the clouds of winter begin
to arrive. These are a different kind of cloud from those of
the early summer; they are grey and lowering, sluggish in
their movements. At all times during the summer, clouds are
about the only feature the sky affords; there are none of the
dust atoms in it that at lower altitudes catch and hold the
sun's rays when it rises and sets. High-country sunrises and
sunsets are seldom colorful. A tinge of pink may color the
sky before the sun rises or vanishes, but that is all.

Clear skies through midsummer days have created a legend that in the Sierra's higher altitudes rain never falls at
night. It is only a legend; the rains are not that selective.
They come both by day and night during the waning of summer, though a midsummer shower, especially during
darkness, is indeed rare. The occasional early-season rains
are welcome, for they speed the snow melt, but late-summer
rains are welcomed even more gratefully, for they end the
time of fire danger, which increases as the duff and meadows
dry.

At both extremes of summer it is easy for those who know
the high country's patterns to distinguish between a sudden
passing shower and a rain that has come to stay a day or
more. Real storms between the snows are as short and turbulent as an adolescent love affair. Such storms arrive virtually
unheralded. They can be seen forming only from the highest
peaks, and their approach is invisible from the slopes they
will pelt.

Arrival of a summer storm is announced by a barrage of
thunder that seldom sounds until a few minutes before the
clouds appear. Lightning follows the first clouds, narrow
sharply defined bolts that shear off the tips of the tallest
pines and run to ground through the tree's moist sap; in ef-

fect, the tree becomes a lightning rod like that on an old-fashioned house or barn. Now and then, a bolt jumps in a spark from tree trunk to duff, and if conditions are dry, the spark ignites the duff. Almost always the rain follows the lightning bolts quickly enough to put out these incipient forest fires. Few of them spread in early summer as they do later in the season when the duff is like tinder and the foliage of the trees is dry. In the early summer the sequence of the storm is quick: thunder and clouds, lightning and rain. Usually in a quarter-hour or so it is over.

Late-summer rains arrive differently and do not unfold as rapidly. They are ushered in by slowly moving clouds that gather in a leisurely fashion around the peaks. From the shrouded heights the clouds creep downward and billow as misty fog over the lower ridges. They form canopies of grey above the valleys and meadows. A few raindrops spatter. There is a lull; then more rain falls, the drops fatter. Another pause, and the real rain begins, gentle but persistent, increasing in intensity, slackening now and then to scattered drops, again increasing, lessening, and finally settling down to a steady fall that continues for half a day or longer.

Birds and animals read the rain signs. They will not interrupt their feeding in the early summer; later in the season they go about their affairs while the preliminary showers are falling, but when the real rain arrives they quickly go to cover. Birds that nest in woodpecker holes, including the woodpeckers themselves, and the chickadees, mountain bluebirds and flycatchers, disappear into their snug homes. The birds who make open nests, in trees or on the ground, continue to sit on their incubating eggs during the short early-summer spatters, but later in the season the warblers, jays, juncos and sparrows perch close to the boles of densely branched whitebarks or Douglas firs or silver pines; they avoid the trees with loose, widely-spaced limbs. No matter how hard the rain is driven by winds into the forest, there are always places near the trunks of close-limbed trees that stay dry.

Animals follow the pattern of the birds. When an early-season shower passes they may huddle in the lee of a big rock or a tree trunk, but later in the summer they disappear soon after the warning drops fall. Chickarees and chipmunks go to their tree holes, ground squirrels and marmots to their burrows, mice to their tunnels. Coyotes and the big cats seek shelter under rock ledges or in crevices, but deer seem to be drawn out by rain and desert their bedding places in the thick brush and go to the meadows to graze. Bears ignore the rain; so do thickly furred predators such as the marten, mink, fisher and weasel. They may well find their best daytime hunting during showers.

Once they arrive, early-summer rains rarely last until nightfall. They stop as they began, unheralded. The rain diminishes in vigor to a few weak spatters. There may be a final flurry as the moving clouds discharge their last drops, then the fall stops. The clouds may stay until the day is almost ended, but usually they lift at sundown. Brief as the shower may have been, the conifers continue to drip through most of the night, and when the sun returns the following morning their dripping goes on until the sun dissolves the clinging drops into mist. The mist veils the meadows, too, for an hour or so, and rises in columns among the trees. Before noon, the air has regained its clarity.

Late-summer rains are neither as gentle nor as predictable as those of the early season. They forewarn by covering the sky slowly with a grey striated blanket that accumulates gradually and sends the temperature swooping down five or six degrees. The clouds do not always release moisture at once. There will be rumbles of thunder and lightning flashes, and these are the dangerous bolts, for the rain may hold off for several days and give fires time to grow. The clouds hold their wet drops stubbornly, through an entire day or even longer. A few lonely raindrops may patter down at dawn, and always there is mist above the lakes and streams in the early-morning hours, but the rain holds off. The clouds appear about to dissolve, then they re-form, but never quite disappear until the summer-ending rain bursts from them without such preliminaries as thunder rolls or warning spatters.

This is cold rain. It does not fall, but rather seems dashed and driven into the dry earth. It pelts the pines, dislodging cones and needles. It denudes the golden aspens of the leaves that have been dancing in bright color since the first cool nights. It sinks into the meadow soil, into the duff, but somehow leaves the surface dry. Rains like these come and go and return again during the final days of summer. They bring a brief revival to meadows that long ago turned yellow; green shoots appear here and there, and on the cold-stripped willows a stray bud or two may appear.

When moisture is restored to the sered soil, the time of frosts begins. Within a few days the meadows go from yellow to brown; the brave green out-of-season shoots are nipped. The frost freezes the grass stems at the point where they emerge from the soil. Dry leaves of skunk cabbage that have been standing, brittle and crackling in the wind, sag in a single night, turn black, topple, and begin to rot the instant they touch the soil. The bushes shed their leaves as the sap in their branches retreats to their roots. The summer is now days, sometimes only hours, from its end.

Even when the brief Sierra summer is observed year after year, there is something almost frightening each season in the rapidity with which it arrives, flourishes and ends.

Only last week, it seems, snow covered both mountainside and meadow. This week, the snow left the meadows and valleys but still clung to the mountain peaks. Yesterday the meadows were wet, glistening, with water shining between grass blades and around the stems of groundsel and mountain buttercups, and in the meadows' low spots rippling snow ponds gleamed. Today the ground is dry between the grass stems; groundsel and buttercups are gone, lupine and larkspur come and gone as well. The snow ponds have vanished, too, sunk into the soil or drained into the streams.

This morning creeks dashed whitely over rocky beds, in afternoon they ran low and shrunken inside their banks, by nightfall they have become scant trickles between the rocks. Tomorrow they will be gone, the stones in their beds dry and covered with fine silt. Next week the meadows will fade from green to yellow; the following week they will be dully brown. The sky will no longer be limitless and blue as it was

A number of big, old trees have rotted from their hearts and toppled to earth.

yesterday, but hidden by low grey clouds pressing down from the ridges. The sun will be hidden and the chilling air will hint of snow.

Calendars and common sense give the summer its true length, and correct the delusions of the senses. Winter in the high country does not begin by calendar and clock, nor does it end by them. Our sensory delusions belie the messages of the devices we have created for measuring the season.

Winter begins to wane when sunset no longer suspends the snow melt and the solemn dripping goes on all night from the trees and rocks and ledges. By the calendar this occurs during the last days of April, the beginning days of May, but the land remains snowbound. True summer starts when green shoots push their way up through the snow, when the earth begins to be bared of its white shroud, and this does not happen until June.

By mid-June the snow is gone from all except sheltered places. Ice on the lakes has broken, the streams are revealed beneath the snowcaps they have worn, and only then does the land begin to pulse with its summer life. At some point after the calendar has passed through most of August, summer starts to fade. There is no overt alteration in weather, no marked change in growth or in the activities of animals and birds; the change is subtle, unnoticed by those who do not know the high country's heartbeat.

Pines continue to thrust out fresh needles and to form cones, but the needles are darker than those which grew so green while the snow was melting, and the cones take shape more quickly. The aspen leaves, bright green on both sides when they first broadened, become dark green on their faces and light silver-olive on their backs, and flash from green to silver as they flutter. The grasses still flourish, but here and there where rock lies below a thin layer of soil, patches of yellow appear and slowly spread where in July there was only green to be seen.

Early blooming wildflowers have already withered, their seeds dropped from hard sepals from which petals have disappeared. Now the dry wildflower stalks rise like exclamation marks above the knee-high grass. Late-blooming flowers come into color, but their petals unfold, blossoms form, become full blown, wither and die, within the span of a few days.

Before July is a week old the animals and birds settle into the routines they follow through summer's remaining days; they begin to build and stock their winter havens. As August fades the animals feed with greater urgency and the filling of food caches takes on a frenzied tempo. The number of small creatures on the meadows has increased. This year's babies have matured during the quick summer weeks, and are establishing their own nests. Early-migrating birds that began arriving before the snow melt are seen in fewer numbers. They are departing day by day to reach warmer places before the high country winter strikes. Still, a few late arrivals show up in August, making brief round trips to feed on the bounty of seeds unlocked from the withering flowers and the dying heavy-headed grasses. They are like the vacationers who come to spend a weekend when the high country seems to pause between the seasons.

Days remain sunny and warm, but the long evening twilight is replaced by a short period of dusk between sunset and night. When the sun vanishes, a chill snaps into the thin air. The nights become sharp as August nears its end; the hours between midnight and dawn find sleepers groping for extra covers or pulling their sleeping bag flaps tighter. August is the month when thundershowers threaten but do not often fulfill their threats.

Suddenly it is September, and overnight the air changes. The thin rime that in mid-August began forming during the dark hours on the ground and grass tips is thicker now, composed of bigger crystals, slower to melt when the sun strikes it after daybreak. The tang that appeared in the air so abruptly becomes a nip, then a bite. By clock-time the sun shows up later each morning and dips earlier behind the ridges. A new voice is heard among the night sounds; wind sighing through the pines overlays the soft earlier notes of rustling branches. The sun loses none of its brilliance, but its warmth is dissipated, absorbed by the thin high clouds through which it now shines on most days.

These high clouds are not the billows of midsummer, which were great fleecy masses sweeping by swiftly, high above the peaks. September's clouds are wispy, nebulous, the kind a child might scratch with chalk upon a blue slate, but the real clouds in the real sky are not chalk-white, they are grey. They hang thinly in motionless layers between sun and mountain tops, never obtrusive, only slightly diminishing the sun's heat and brilliance, almost always present.

Birds and small animals are fewer now; they are adjusting

their lives to the season's change. Except for the sparrows, small birds vanish, and even the numbers of the jays and robins decrease. Hawks no longer soar high but skim only a few yards above the grass tops. Ground squirrels heed their hibernating instinct and more of them disappear into their burrows each day until one day all of them are gone. Chipmunks diminish in numbers. Most of them are now second-litter babies, born in early August, precociously matured, setting up their own nests and food caches. Chickarees are busier than they were when preparing for the birth of their litters in early summer; they gather fresh nesting material to reline their hideaways before the cold days arrive.

Marten and mink no longer confine their movements to the darkest hours, but come out before dusk and stay active until the sun begins to flood the groves with light. Weasels, their brown coats beginning to fade to the white they will wear through the months of snow, bound at high noon across the meadow, seeking the field mice that still use their runs among the grass roots.

Deer bed down later in the morning and leave their brush-hidden sleeping places before dusk. The big predators are not as wary as they were about coming out in daylight; they must spend longer hours hunting now that small game has become scarce. The bears are driven to eat until their bellies bulge; they are huge with layers of fat under gleaming fur, though they will not begin to hibernate until long after the heavier snowfalls of December and January have piled up to seal the high granite completely. The cougars that do not share the habit or instinct that keeps most of them above timberline all year begin their long stealthy journey to the foothills. None of these changes occur overnight; each species adjusts to its own calendar in changing its summer habits.

Underfoot the ground becomes more noisy. Long dry days have driven all the moisture from the duff on the forest floor; its thick layer of pine needles no longer yields softly when a foot comes down on it, but crackles and snaps. The pines remain green, but undergo an impalpable change; their needles darken and lose resiliency as their sap drains off into the roots. The pine branches no longer whisper in the wind but groan sadly and pop now and then in muffled miniature explosions. Overnight the aspen leaves go from green to gold and again overnight from gold to orange; they still dance when a wind passes, but it is a slow pavane instead of a sprightly jig, and with each stirring a few leaves flutter down from each tree.

On the slopes the dogwood blazes red among the twigged skeletons of lesser bushes that have already lost their foliage. In meadows the sered grass rustles loudly; it does not sway gently with the breeze, but flattens noisily to earth. The few streams that still flow shrink to threads. Around lake edges the water pulls away from the miniscule ripples its wavelets earlier formed in the shoreline; the lakes are dwindling now that they are no longer fed by melting snow and tuneful creeks.

As the winds grow from gentle zephyrs to brisk breezes the few small animals that are yet abroad stay even closer to their shelters. No matter how keenly attuned their senses are to the normal voices of forest or clearing or meadow, the new dimension of sound the wind now creates masks the movements of hunters or the rustling approach of ground-bound ferals, and the thin clouds shroud and blur the shadows of cruising hawks. The small creatures get a respite at times when the wind is hard and shifting. Hawks do not bother to fly at such times, for in the always-moving grass even their keen eyes cannot distinguish the small disturbances that mark the passage of a ground squirrel or mouse. The hawks perch hungry on days of high wind, their feathers ruffled and their heads pulled close to their bodies, as they wait for the wind to die.

It is the wind that tells of summer's end. Since June it has been steady, changing direction only slightly, coming always from the south or southwest. One day in September it begins to gust and veer, and after each succeeding lull its direction changes just a bit until from south it has moved in steps through west, northwest, and finally to north, where it settles down. The intermittent gusting will go on for three days, four, five; between each period of flurrying winds the days are calm, but after each time of calm when the wind returns it blows with increased vigor. These are the winds that bring in low stratified clouds, grey in their lowest layers and shading lighter with each layer until the topmost white is reached. These are the clouds that slide just above the peaks.

Sunshine vanishes or is obscured and the wind blows colder. Under its constant rough caress the ground begins to chill. Nightfall comes earlier than ever with the sun hidden

Silence sifts down with the falling snow. One season has died while another is being reborn.

behind clouds. One night there is a preliminary pattering of
rain, a few drops tapping on the dry pine needles that lie
atop the forest duff, spattering when broken by the dry
stems of meadow grass. The rain cools the earth even more
quickly than the wind. Soon the tapping stops and there is
silence. The snow has begun to fall.

Big flakes swirl down over the high peaks first, borne by
dying breezes; then the flakes start a slow creeping down the
flanks of mountains. The flakes fall thickly, but melt quickly
when they touch trees or soil; both of these still hold a
residue of warmth. On the high granite, which is never more
than surface-warm, the snow does not melt. It nestles in
sheltered crevices and fills them, carrying a fresh chill deep
into the rock. The rough surface of the granite grows colder
as the nights lengthen and the snow continues to fall. Invisibly now, air chilled by the granite flows down the slopes to
prepare the forest and meadows to receive the snow.

Surrounded by the ever seeping, ever flowing, ever colder
air, the thin pine needles lose the warmth they have
retained. They hold the snow instead of melting it, and the
trees become crested in white. On both rocky tors and pines
the flakes cling thinly and tentatively when they first fall, a
light dusting. On the meadows the flakes do not cling at all,
but sift down through dry slim grass stems to melt on soil
still warm at the grasses' roots.

Persistently the snow settles from low-hanging clouds,
heavy now with moisture they have carried from the western
ocean. The flakes soon find lodging on the heads of meadow
grass and pile higher on the pine boughs. Within hours the
snow weighs down the long delicate grass stems, bends their
heads to the ground. The meadows, which have appeared as
expanses of ochre studded with white tufts, now become
completely white.

Before this has happened the pines are thickly covered.
Their limbs sag under an increasing burden of wet, heavy
flakes. They shed this first covering easily when the wind
blows, as it does from time to time, but during the brief contact between snow and needles the fractional warmth left in
the trees melts the snow minutely. When the blobs fall off

the limbs they leave the needles coated with a thin film of moisture, and the instant the needles are bared the cold air turns this moisture into ice. Now the snowflakes that are still falling find a firm anchorage. They cling and will not be dislodged again, nor will they melt. The pines will wear white now through the rest of winter.

In unsheltered places the first snow may go when touched even briefly by a vagrant warm breeze or a chance sunray, but it has been a warning, and nature seldom warns twice. Small animals hurry to their nests where they will now remain, emerging only to visit their food caches. The birds that have not yet migrated depart. The deer abandon their beds and begin to move with a faster pace toward the foothills and valleys, their russet coats wet-beaded as snowflakes settle on their warm bodies and quickly melt.

Silence sifts down with the falling snow. One season has died while another was being reborn. Now the high country will live a slower, more secret life, until the constantly changing cycles shift and the short Sierra summer returns.